Copyright © 2024 by NovoLit Publishing

All rights reserved. No part of this book may be reproduced, distributed, or transmitted in any form or by any means, including photocopying, recording, or other electronic or mechanical methods, without the prior written permission of the publisher, except in the case of brief quotations embodied in critical reviews and certain other noncommercial uses permitted by copyright

ISBN: 9798329943214

Printed in the United States of America

Cover design by Art Painter

Dedication

To all the hardworking professionals who tirelessly strive for excellence, balance, and well-being in their careers. This book is dedicated to you—the unsung heroes of the modern workplace who face challenges with resilience and determination.

To the leaders who strive to create supportive environments, the employees who seek balance amidst their daily challenges, and the organizations committed to fostering well-being and productivity.

To all those who navigate the complexities of the modern workplace with resilience and determination.

This book is for you.

May it serve as a beacon of guidance, support, and inspiration in your journey toward mastering stress and achieving success, both at work and beyond.

"It's not the load that breaks you down, it's the way you carry it."

LOU HOLTZ

Contents

Introduction: *Page 06*

Section 01: Understanding Workplace Stress   *Page 08*

Section 02: The Science Behind Stress and Mental Health   *Page 18*

Section 03: Strategies for Identifying Stress Triggers   *Page 27*

Section 04: Effective Stress Management Techniques   *Page 34*

Section 05: Promoting Work-Life Balance   *Page 42*

Section 06: Mindfulness and Meditation Practices   *Page 46*

Section 07: Physical Health and Stress Reduction   *Page 61*

Section 08: Effective Communication and Conflict Resolution   *Page 68*

Section 09: Leadership's Role in Stress Management   *Page 77*

Section 10: Building Resilience and Adaptability   *Page 84*

Section 11: Technology and Stress: Finding Balance   *Page 93*

Section 12: Cultural and Organizational Influences on Stress   *Page 103*

Section 13: Self-Care and Personal Well-being   *Page 113*

Section 14: Legal and Ethical Considerations in Stress Management   *Page 123*

Section 15: Conclusion: Sustaining Well-being Beyond Work   *Page 134*

Concluding Section: Final Thoughts and Call to Action   *Page 142*

Preface

Welcome to "Mastering Stress at Work: Strategies for Success." In today's fast-paced world, managing workplace stress is essential for both personal and organizational well-being. This book is your guide to navigating stress effectively, offering practical strategies to improve communication, resolve conflicts, and foster a positive work environment.

Whether you're an employee aiming to enhance your professional life or a leader dedicated to creating a supportive workplace, the insights and action steps provided will help you thrive. Implementing these strategies will not only boost individual well-being but also drive organizational success.

 Thank you for joining us on this journey to a healthier, more productive work life.

Sincerely,

JOHNATHAN MILLER

Introduction

Imagine waking up each morning feeling energized and eager to tackle the day ahead. You stride into your workplace with a clear mind, knowing that you have the tools and strategies to handle whatever challenges come your way. Stress no longer dictates your productivity, mood, or overall well-being. Instead, you feel balanced, focused, and in control.

But let's face it: for many of us, this scenario feels more like a distant dream than a daily reality. The modern workplace is a breeding ground for stress, with its relentless demands, tight deadlines, and ever-increasing expectations. You may feel overwhelmed by an endless to-do list, anxious about upcoming projects, or frustrated by workplace conflicts. The constant pressure can take a toll on your mental and physical health, leading to burnout, decreased productivity, and even strained relationships both at work and at home.

Now, envision a different future—one where you have mastered the art of managing stress effectively. By reading this book, you'll gain the insights and tools necessary to transform your work life. Imagine confidently navigating your responsibilities, maintaining a healthy work-life balance, and fostering a supportive, positive work environment. You'll learn to turn stress into a catalyst for growth rather than a roadblock to success.

In "Mastering Stress at Work: Strategies for Success," you will discover:

- **Understanding Workplace Stress:** Gain a deep understanding of the common stressors in professional environments and their impact on productivity and mental health.
- **The Science Behind Stress and Mental Health:** Explore the psychological and physiological aspects of stress and the importance of mental health awareness.

- **Effective Stress Management Techniques:** Learn proven strategies for immediate stress relief and sustainable stress reduction.
- **Mindfulness and Meditation Practices:** Incorporate mindfulness into your daily routine and utilize guided meditation exercises for stress relief.
- **Effective Communication and Conflict Resolution:** Improve your communication skills and handle workplace conflicts constructively.
- **Leadership's Role in Stress Management:** Understand the responsibilities of leaders in promoting employee well-being and creating a supportive work environment.
- **Legal and Ethical Considerations in Stress Management:** Know your legal rights and protections related to workplace stress and the ethical responsibilities of organizations.
- **Physical Health and Stress Reduction:** Discover the impact of physical activity on stress levels and ergonomic tips for reducing physical stress at work.
- **Conclusion: Sustaining Well-being Beyond Work:** Recap key strategies, encourage continued growth, and provide actionable steps for achieving balance and success in the workplace.

This book is not just another guide on stress management. It is a comprehensive, actionable blueprint for transforming your work life. By committing to reading and implementing the strategies outlined in this book, you are taking a crucial step toward a healthier, more balanced, and fulfilling professional life. Don't let stress control you—take control of your stress and unlock your full potential at work. Your journey to mastering stress starts here.

Section 01

Understanding Workplace Stress

Introduction to Workplace Stress

Workplace stress is an increasingly common issue that significantly impacts both individuals and organizations. It manifests as a physical or emotional response to work-related pressures and challenges. When left unchecked, workplace stress can lead to severe health problems and decreased productivity. Understanding the roots of workplace stress and its effects is the first step toward managing and mitigating it effectively.

Common Workplace Stressors

Workplace stressors are numerous and varied, often depending on the specific environment and individual roles. Here are some of the most prevalent stressors in a professional environment:

1. Deadlines and Workload

- **Impact of Tight Deadlines**: Constantly working under tight deadlines can cause significant stress, leading to anxiety and burnout. Employees may feel pressured to rush through tasks, increasing the likelihood of mistakes and reducing overall job satisfaction.
    - *Example*: An employee in a marketing firm consistently faced tight deadlines for campaign launches. This resulted in late nights and weekends spent working, which eventually led to burnout and decreased job performance.
- **Managing Excessive Workloads**: Balancing a heavy workload can be overwhelming. When employees are given more tasks than they can handle, it results in prolonged stress and decreased productivity.
    - *Example*: A software developer was assigned multiple projects simultaneously without adequate support. The overwhelming workload caused chronic

stress, impacting their mental health and leading to a significant drop in productivity.

2. Interpersonal Conflicts

- **Conflicts with Colleagues or Supervisors**: Disagreements and conflicts at work can create a tense and hostile environment. This not only affects mental health but also hampers team collaboration and productivity.
  - *Case Study*: At a mid-sized company, unresolved conflicts between team members led to a toxic work environment. The team's productivity plummeted as employees avoided communication and collaboration. After implementing conflict resolution training and promoting open communication, the team saw a significant improvement in both morale and productivity.

3. Low Salaries

- **Financial Stress**: Insufficient compensation is a major source of stress, particularly when employees struggle to meet their financial obligations. This stress can spill over into their work performance and overall job satisfaction.
  - *Statistics*: According to the American Psychological Association (APA), 66% of adults cite money as a significant source of stress. Additionally, low salaries contribute to higher turnover rates and lower job satisfaction.

4. Few Opportunities for Growth or Advancement

- **Career Stagnation**: Lack of growth opportunities can lead to frustration and a feeling of being stuck. Employees who don't see a path to advancement may lose motivation and disengage from their work.
  - *Example*: An employee in a customer service role felt undervalued and stuck in their position. Without clear career progression, their motivation dwindled, leading to increased absenteeism and decreased performance.

5. Work that Isn't Engaging or Challenging

- **Monotonous Tasks**: Performing repetitive and unchallenging tasks can lead to boredom and disengagement, contributing to stress.
    - *Example*: An administrative assistant found their daily tasks monotonous and unchallenging. This lack of engagement led to stress and a feeling of being unfulfilled at work.
- **Finding Engagement**: Strategies for finding motivation and engagement in mundane work, such as setting personal goals and seeking opportunities for skill development.

6. Lack of Social Support

- **Importance of a Supportive Environment**: Social support from colleagues and supervisors can significantly reduce stress. A lack of such support can make work feel isolating and overwhelming.
    - *Examples*: Real-life instances where social support helped mitigate stress, such as a company implementing a mentorship program to foster supportive relationships among employees.

7. Not Having Enough Control Over Job-Related Decisions

- **Autonomy and Stress**: Lack of control over one's work can be a major stressor. Employees who feel they have no say in their tasks or processes may experience higher stress levels.
    - *Increasing Control*: Techniques to increase autonomy and involvement in decision-making, such as involving employees in goal-setting and encouraging feedback.

8. Conflicting Demands or Unclear Performance Expectations

- **Unclear Job Expectations**: When employees are unsure of their roles or receive conflicting demands, it creates confusion and stress.

- - *Seeking Clarity*: How to clarify roles and manage expectations to reduce stress, including regular check-ins with supervisors and clear communication of goals.

9. Poor Management and Work Design

- **Role of Management**: Poor management practices and lack of leadership can create a stressful work environment.
  - *Examples of Poor Work Design*: Insights into how inadequate work design contributes to stress, such as unrealistic performance targets or lack of resources.

10. Task Design

- **Factors Affecting Task Design**: Workload, pace, variety, meaningfulness, and autonomy play crucial roles in employee stress levels.
  - *Ensuring Adequate Time*: The importance of giving employees sufficient time to complete tasks and how task design impacts stress levels.

11. Shiftwork/Hours of Work

- **Irregular Hours**: Shift work and irregular hours can disrupt an employee's routine and sleep patterns, leading to increased stress.
  - *Managing Work Schedules*: Strategies for coping with irregular work hours, including maintaining a consistent sleep schedule and using relaxation techniques.

12. Skills/Abilities Mismatch

- **Job Demands vs. Skills**: A mismatch between an employee's skills and job demands can lead to stress and frustration.
  - *Importance of Training*: Providing adequate training and preparation to meet job requirements and how this reduces stress.

13. Lack of Appreciation

- **Feeling Valued**: Not feeling appreciated can negatively affect an employee's morale and increase stress.
  - *Fostering Appreciation*: Ways to create a culture of appreciation in the workplace, such as regular recognition and reward programs.

14. Isolation at the Workplace

- **Emotional Isolation**: Working alone or feeling emotionally isolated can be a significant stressor.
  - *Building Connections*: Importance of social interactions and team-building activities in mitigating stress.

The Impact of Workplace Stress on Productivity and Mental Health

Workplace stress has far-reaching consequences, affecting both individual well-being and organizational efficiency. Here are some key statistics and impacts:

1. Statistics and Data

- Nearly one in five US adults live with a mental illness.
- Workplace stress causes 120,000 deaths annually in the US.
- 83% of US workers suffer from work-related stress.
- 54% of workers report that work stress affects their home life.
- For every $1 spent on mental health, employers see a $4 return in productivity gains.
- 13.7 million working days are lost annually in the UK due to work-related stress.
- 44% of people globally experience significant workplace stress daily.

2. Consequences of Workplace Stress

- **Absenteeism and Turnover Rates**: High-stress levels lead to increased absenteeism and higher turnover rates, which can be costly for organizations.

- *Example*: A large corporation experienced a 20% increase in turnover due to stress-related burnout, leading to significant recruitment and training costs.
- **Decreased Productivity and Job Performance**: Stress hampers an employee's ability to focus, make decisions, and perform effectively.
  - *Example*: A team of software engineers showed a 30% decline in productivity when stress levels were high, affecting project timelines and quality.
- **Impact on Mental Health**: Chronic stress can lead to severe mental health issues such as anxiety, depression, and burnout.
  - *Statistics*: 51% of adults who felt stressed reported feeling depressed, and 61% reported feeling anxious.

Case Study: The Impact of Workplace Stress on a Financial Services Firm

In a mid-sized financial services firm, the pressures of tight deadlines and high workloads were taking a toll on employees. The company faced a high turnover rate, with many employees citing stress and burnout as their reasons for leaving.

Background

- The firm had a demanding work culture with long hours and constant pressure to meet targets.
- Employees reported feeling overwhelmed by their workloads and the lack of support from management.

Effects of Stress

- **High Turnover**: The firm experienced a 25% annual turnover rate, significantly higher than the industry average.
- **Decreased Productivity**: Stress led to a 15% decline in overall productivity, impacting the firm's bottom line.
- **Health Issues**: Several employees reported health issues related to stress, including anxiety and depression.

Intervention

- The firm implemented a comprehensive stress management program, including regular workshops on stress reduction techniques, increased support from management, and flexible work arrangements.
- A mentorship program was established to provide employees with additional support and guidance.

Results

- **Reduced Turnover**: The turnover rate decreased by 10% in the first year after implementing the program.
- **Improved Productivity**: Productivity levels increased by 20%, as employees felt more supported and less stressed.
- **Better Health Outcomes**: Employees reported fewer health issues and an overall improvement in well-being.

Actionable Insights for Managing Workplace Stress

Managing workplace stress requires a multifaceted approach that addresses both individual and organizational factors. Here are some actionable insights to help identify and mitigate workplace stress:

1. Track Your Stressors

- **Keeping a Journal**: Identify patterns and triggers by recording stressful situations and reactions. This helps in understanding the root causes of stress.
  - *Tip*: Note down the time, situation, people involved, and your emotional response to identify trends and common stressors.

2. Develop Healthy Responses

- **Exercise and Hobbies**: Engage in physical activity and leisure activities to reduce stress. Exercise helps in releasing endorphins, which improve mood and reduce stress.
  - *Example*: A daily 30-minute walk can significantly lower stress levels.

- **Quality Sleep**: Ensure adequate sleep by limiting caffeine and minimizing screen time before bed. Good sleep hygiene practices can help improve sleep quality.
  - *Tip*: Establish a regular sleep schedule and create a calming bedtime routine.

3. Establish Boundaries

- **Work-Life Boundaries**: Set rules to separate work from personal life, such as not checking emails after hours. Clear boundaries help in preventing work from encroaching on personal time.
  - *Example*: A software engineer stopped checking work emails after 7 PM, which improved their work-life balance and reduced stress.

4. Take Time to Recharge

- **Disconnecting from Work**: Regularly take breaks and vacations to rejuvenate and prevent burnout. Time away from work can help in recharging and gaining a fresh perspective.
  - *Example*: A marketing manager took a week off every quarter to unwind and return to work with renewed energy.

5. Learn How to Relax

- **Relaxation Techniques**: Practice meditation, deep breathing, and mindfulness to alleviate stress. These techniques can help in calming the mind and reducing anxiety.
  - *Tip*: Spend 10 minutes each day practicing deep breathing or meditation.

6. Talk to Your Supervisor

- **Open Communication**: Discuss stressors with your supervisor to find solutions and get necessary support. Open dialogue can help in identifying and addressing stressors.
  - *Example*: A customer service representative discussed their workload with their supervisor and received additional support, reducing their stress levels.

7. Get Some Support

- **Employee Assistance Programs**: Utilize available resources for stress management and professional help. These programs can provide counseling and support for dealing with stress.
  - *Tip*: Check if your organization offers employee assistance programs or mental health resources.

8. Psychological Detachment from Work

- **Mental Disconnection**: Techniques to mentally switch off from work-related thoughts, such as engaging in hobbies or spending time with family and friends.
  - *Example*: A project manager used their commute home to listen to audiobooks, helping them detach from work thoughts.

9. Harnessing Micro-Breaks

- **Short Breaks**: The benefits of taking brief breaks throughout the workday to maintain focus and reduce stress. Micro-breaks can help in recharging and improving concentration.
  - *Tip*: Take a 5-minute break every hour to stretch and move around.

10. Prioritize High-Effort Recovery Activities

- **Effective Stress Reduction**: Engage in activities that significantly lower stress levels, such as physical exercise or creative pursuits.
  - *Example*: An accountant took up painting as a hobby, which helped in reducing stress and improving mental health.

11. Shaping Your Environment

- **Work Environment**: Create a conducive work environment that promotes well-being and reduces stress. A well-designed workspace can enhance comfort and productivity.

- Tip: Personalize your workspace with items that make you happy, such as plants or photos.

12. Socializing with Co-Workers

- **Building Social Connections**: Importance of social interactions and team activities in mitigating stress. Building strong relationships with colleagues can provide emotional support.
  - *Example*: A team held regular social events to strengthen bonds and reduce stress.

13. Self-Kindness and Regular Exercise

- **Self-Care and Physical Activity**: Emphasize self-kindness and maintain a regular exercise routine. Taking care of oneself is crucial for managing stress.
  - *Tip*: Practice self-compassion and engage in regular physical activity, such as yoga or running.

14. Scheduling Breaks and Relaxation Techniques

- **Regular Breaks**: Ensure frequent breaks and practice relaxation techniques for effective stress management. Taking regular breaks can help in maintaining energy levels and focus.
  - *Tip*: Schedule short breaks throughout the day to practice relaxation techniques, such as deep breathing or stretching.

Conclusion

Understanding the various stressors in the workplace and their impact is crucial for developing effective strategies to manage and reduce stress. By implementing the actionable insights provided, individuals and organizations can create a healthier, more productive work environment. Remember, addressing workplace stress is not just about improving productivity; it's about enhancing overall well-being and creating a supportive, fulfilling workplace for everyone.

The Science Behind Stress and Mental Health

Introduction

Stress is an inevitable part of life, particularly in the fast-paced and demanding environments of modern workplaces. While short-term stress can enhance performance by providing a burst of energy and focus, chronic stress has far-reaching implications for both mental and physical health. This section explores the intricate science behind stress, its psychological and physiological aspects, the neurological impacts of chronic stress, and the critical importance of mental health awareness in the workplace. By understanding these elements, we can develop effective strategies to mitigate stress and promote a healthier, more productive work environment.

1. Psychological and Physiological Aspects of Stress

Psychological Aspects:

- **Emotional Responses**: Stress triggers a wide range of emotional responses that can significantly affect an individual's mental well-being. Common emotional reactions include anxiety, irritability, and depression. When stress becomes chronic, these feelings can intensify and lead to more severe mental health issues such as generalized anxiety disorder and major depressive disorder.
    - *Example*: A comprehensive study by the American Psychological Association revealed that employees experiencing high levels of workplace stress reported significantly higher levels of anxiety and depression compared to those with lower stress levels. This correlation underscores the direct link between workplace stress and emotional health.
- **Cognitive Effects**: Stress can impair cognitive functions such as attention, memory, and decision-making. When under stress, individuals may find it challenging to concentrate, remember information, or make sound decisions.

- *Example*: Research indicates that individuals subjected to chronic workplace stress often exhibit decreased cognitive performance, which can impact their productivity and ability to perform tasks effectively.

Physiological Aspects:

- **Fight-or-Flight Response**: The fight-or-flight response is the body's immediate reaction to perceived threats, involving a cascade of hormonal changes designed to prepare the body for action. This response, regulated by the hypothalamus, prompts the adrenal glands to release adrenaline and cortisol. These hormones increase heart rate, blood pressure, and glucose levels, providing a burst of energy and heightened alertness.
  - *Example*: While the fight-or-flight response is beneficial in acute situations, its chronic activation can lead to detrimental health effects. Prolonged exposure to cortisol can suppress the immune system, increase blood pressure, and elevate the risk of chronic diseases such as cardiovascular disease and diabetes.
- **Hormonal Changes**: Stress induces significant hormonal changes in the body, particularly involving cortisol, the primary stress hormone. Elevated cortisol levels over extended periods can disrupt various bodily functions, leading to serious health consequences.
  - *Statistic*: Chronic stress has been linked to consistently high levels of cortisol, which can impair cognitive function, increase abdominal fat, and elevate blood pressure. Research indicates that individuals with high stress levels are more likely to suffer from cognitive impairments and physical health issues related to hormonal imbalances.
- **Physical Symptoms**: Chronic stress manifests in various physical symptoms, including headaches, muscle tension, fatigue, and gastrointestinal issues. These symptoms can further exacerbate stress, creating a vicious cycle of physical and mental health problems.

- *Example*: A survey by the American Institute of Stress found that 77% of individuals regularly experience physical symptoms caused by stress, highlighting the pervasive impact of stress on overall health.

2. Neurological Effects of Chronic Stress

Brain Structure and Function:

- **Hippocampus**: The hippocampus, a critical brain region for memory and learning, is particularly vulnerable to the effects of chronic stress. High levels of cortisol can cause atrophy in the hippocampus, leading to memory problems and cognitive decline.
  - *Example*: Neuroimaging studies have shown that individuals exposed to prolonged stress often exhibit reduced hippocampal volume and impaired memory function. This effect is particularly pronounced in people with chronic stress-related disorders such as PTSD and depression.
- **Prefrontal Cortex**: The prefrontal cortex, responsible for decision-making, problem-solving, and emotional regulation, is also affected by chronic stress. Prolonged stress can reduce the volume of the prefrontal cortex, impairing executive functions.
  - *Statistic*: Research indicates that chronic stress can lead to a decrease in prefrontal cortex volume, resulting in difficulties with tasks that require complex thinking, planning, and emotional regulation. This can significantly impact an individual's ability to function effectively in both personal and professional settings.

Neurotransmitter Levels:

- **Serotonin and Dopamine**: Stress affects the levels of key neurotransmitters such as serotonin and dopamine, which play crucial roles in regulating mood and pleasure. Imbalances in these neurotransmitters can lead to mood disorders and decreased motivation.

- *Statistic*: Chronic stress is associated with reduced levels of serotonin and dopamine, contributing to conditions such as depression and anhedonia (the inability to feel pleasure). These neurotransmitter imbalances highlight the profound impact of stress on mental health.
- **Neuroplasticity**: Chronic stress can impair neuroplasticity, the brain's ability to adapt and reorganize itself. This can hinder the brain's capacity to recover from trauma and maintain cognitive functions.
  - *Example*: Studies have shown that individuals with chronic stress exhibit decreased neuroplasticity, which can result in long-term cognitive deficits and reduced resilience to future stressors.

3. Importance of Mental Health Awareness in the Workplace

Mental Health Training and Programs:

- **Employee Training**: Providing mental health training for employees is essential for fostering a supportive workplace environment. Training can help employees recognize signs of stress and mental health issues, promoting early intervention and support.
  - *Example*: Companies that implement comprehensive mental health training programs report improved employee well-being and productivity. For instance, a tech company that introduced mental health training saw a significant reduction in stress-related absenteeism and an increase in employee engagement.
- **Leadership Training**: Training leaders to recognize and address mental health issues is crucial. Leaders who understand the importance of mental health can create a supportive work environment and lead by example.
  - *Example*: A manufacturing firm that trained its managers in mental health awareness saw a marked improvement in employee morale and a reduction in stress-related incidents. This underscores the importance of leadership in fostering a mentally healthy workplace.

Stigma Reduction Programs:

- **Creating an Open Culture**: Reducing stigma around mental health is crucial for encouraging employees to seek help. Promoting open discussions about mental health can create a supportive workplace culture where employees feel comfortable addressing their mental health needs.
    - *Statistic*: Organizations with active mental health awareness campaigns see a 20% increase in employees accessing mental health resources. This highlights the positive impact of reducing stigma on employee well-being.
- **Mental Health Ambassadors**: Designating mental health ambassadors within the organization can help normalize conversations about mental health and provide peer support.
    - *Example*: A financial services company introduced a mental health ambassador program, resulting in increased mental health resource utilization and improved employee satisfaction.

Support Resources:

- **Employee Assistance Programs (EAPs)**: EAPs provide confidential counselling and support services to employees dealing with stress and mental health issues. These programs offer a range of resources, including counselling, legal and financial advice, and wellness programs.
    - *Example*: A large corporation that introduced a comprehensive EAP saw a 30% reduction in absenteeism and a significant improvement in employee satisfaction scores. This demonstrates the effectiveness of providing accessible support resources.
- **Wellness Initiatives**: Implementing wellness initiatives such as on-site fitness centres, mindfulness programs, and stress management workshops can significantly reduce workplace stress.
    - *Example*: A healthcare company introduced a wellness initiative that included yoga classes, meditation sessions, and nutrition counselling. Employees reported reduced stress levels and improved overall well-being.

4. Case Studies and Real-Life Examples

Case Study: High-Stress Work Environment

- **Scenario**: A tech company faced high turnover rates due to stress from demanding deadlines and heavy workloads. Employees reported feeling overwhelmed and burned out.
    - *Intervention*: The company introduced flexible work hours, mental health days, and regular stress management workshops.
    - *Outcome*: Turnover rates decreased by 25%, and employee satisfaction scores increased by 40%. This case study illustrates the positive impact of addressing workplace stress through targeted interventions.

Example: Mental Health Awareness Campaign

- **Scenario**: A manufacturing firm launched a mental health awareness campaign to reduce stigma and encourage employees to seek help.
    - *Intervention*: The campaign included workshops, mental health first aid training, and visible support from leadership.
    - *Outcome*: The firm saw a 50% increase in employees using mental health resources and a significant drop in stress-related absenteeism. This example underscores the importance of proactive mental health initiatives.

Detailed Case Study: Consequences of Workplace Stress

- **Scenario**: A financial services firm experienced high levels of stress among employees, leading to decreased productivity and increased absenteeism. The primary stressors were tight deadlines, a high workload, and a lack of support from management.
    - *Intervention*: The firm conducted a comprehensive stress audit to identify the main sources of stress. Based on the findings, they implemented several measures, including:

- Establishing a clear communication channel between employees and management.
        - Introducing flexible work arrangements and remote work options.
        - Providing training on stress management techniques, such as mindfulness and time management.
        - Offering regular wellness programs, including yoga and meditation sessions.
        - Enhancing the Employee Assistance Program (EAP) to provide more accessible mental health support.
    - *Outcome*: Within six months, the firm saw a 30% reduction in stress-related absenteeism and a 20% increase in employee productivity. Employee surveys indicated a significant improvement in job satisfaction and overall well-being. This case study highlights the importance of a holistic approach to managing workplace stress and its positive impact on both employees and the organization.

5. Actionable Insights

Strategies for Managing Stress:

- **Promote Healthy Work-Life Balance**: Encourage employees to set boundaries between work and personal life to reduce stress and prevent burnout.
    - *Tip*: Implement policies that support flexible work schedules and remote work options. Encourage employees to take regular breaks and utilize their vacation time.
- **Regular Mental Health Check-Ins**: Conduct regular check-ins with employees to discuss their mental health and stress levels. This can help identify issues early and provide necessary support.
    - *Tip*: Train managers to recognize signs of stress and provide appropriate support. Consider implementing a buddy system where employees can support each other.

- **Create a Supportive Environment**: Foster a workplace culture that values mental health and provides resources for stress management.
  - *Tip*: Offer access to counselling services, stress management workshops, and relaxation spaces. Encourage open communication about mental health and create an environment where employees feel safe discussing their concerns.

Additional Recommendations:

- **Encourage Physical Activity**: Promote regular physical activity as a way to reduce stress. Physical exercise can improve mood, boost energy levels, and enhance overall well-being.
  - *Example*: Implement workplace wellness programs that include fitness challenges, on-site gym facilities, or discounted gym memberships.
- **Provide Mindfulness and Meditation Resources**: Mindfulness and meditation practices can help employees manage stress and improve focus. Consider offering mindfulness workshops or providing access to meditation apps.
  - *Example*: A financial services company introduced weekly mindfulness sessions, resulting in improved employee focus and reduced stress levels.
- **Support Social Connections**: Encourage social interactions and team-building activities to foster a sense of community and support among employees.
  - *Example*: Organize regular team-building events, social gatherings, or virtual coffee breaks to strengthen employee relationships.

Encouraging a Growth Mindset:

- **Foster Resilience**: Encourage employees to develop a growth mindset, where challenges are seen as opportunities for learning and growth. This can enhance their ability to cope with stress and adapt to changes.
  - *Tip*: Provide training on resilience-building techniques, such as setting realistic goals, maintaining a positive outlook, and learning from setbacks.

- **Promote Continuous Learning**: Offer opportunities for professional development and continuous learning. Engaging in new learning experiences can help employees feel more competent and confident, reducing stress levels.
  - *Example*: A tech company that invested in employee development programs saw increased job satisfaction and reduced stress among its workforce.

Conclusion

Understanding the science behind stress and its impact on mental health is crucial for creating a supportive and productive work environment. By recognizing the psychological, physiological, and neurological effects of stress, organizations can implement effective strategies to manage it and promote mental health awareness. Prioritizing mental health in the workplace not only improves employee well-being but also enhances overall productivity and job satisfaction. Implementing these insights and recommendations can lead to a healthier, happier, and more resilient workforce. Through continued efforts to understand and address workplace stress, we can create environments where employees thrive and organizations succeed.

Advanced Journaling and Reflective Writing

Personal Stress Triggers

- **Emotional Reactions:** Reflect on emotional responses (e.g., frustration, anxiety) to pinpoint recurring stress triggers and their intensity. Explore how specific situations or interactions provoke emotional reactions.

  Tip: Consider using descriptive language to articulate the intensity of these emotions, making an effort to understand their potential cause of stress.

  Example: Journal about your feelings of anxiety when preparing for an important presentation at work. Explore the specific aspects of preparation that trigger these emotions, such as fear of failure or uncertainty about the audience's response.

- **Thought Patterns:** Analyze cognitive patterns (e.g., perfectionism, self-criticism) that contribute to stress. Challenge irrational beliefs and identify realistic perspectives to mitigate their impact on stress levels.

  Tip: Write down your thoughts as they occur, and then review them to identify patterns of thought that contribute to your stress.

  Example: Notice how you consistently criticize yourself for perceived mistakes at work. Challenge these thoughts by considering alternative explanations or more balanced perspectives.

- **Physical Symptoms:** Document physical manifestations of stress (e.g., headaches, muscle tension) to identify physiological cues and their correlation with stress triggers. Monitor changes in physical health during stressful periods.

  Tip: Keep a detailed record of your physical symptoms, noting the circumstances under which they occur to identify patterns.

  Example: Track your sleep patterns and headaches during periods of high workload. Note any changes in these patterns as workload intensity varies.

- **Event-Trigger Analysis:** Review journal entries to identify common themes or events preceding stress episodes:

- Work Assignments: Note tasks or projects associated with heightened stress levels. Identify patterns in workload distribution or deadlines that contribute to stress. Document specific instances where workload exceeded capacity.

  Tip: Use bullet points to list specific tasks or deadlines that caused stress, along with the reasons why they caused stress.

  Example: Document instances where tight deadlines led to stress, detailing the tasks involved and the pressure felt to meet them.

- Interpersonal Interactions: Analyze interactions with colleagues or clients that evoke stress reactions. Note communication challenges, conflicts, or expectations that trigger stress responses. Document instances of miscommunication or conflict resolution challenges.

  Tip: Describe specific interactions that have caused stress, including what was said and how you felt during and after the interaction.

  Example: Journal about a meeting where a disagreement with a colleague escalated into a stressful conflict, affecting your mood and productivity.

- Environmental Factors: Assess workplace conditions (e.g., noise levels, lighting) that influence stress levels. Document environmental triggers and their impact on emotional well-being. Identify specific environmental changes that exacerbate or alleviate stress.

  Tip: Make note of changes in your environment, such as office renovations or new equipment, that have affected your stress levels.

  Example: Record how changes in office layout and noise levels have influenced your ability to concentrate and manage stress effectively.

Mindfulness Practices

Body Scan Meditation: Practice body scan meditation to enhance awareness of physical sensations linked to stress:

- **Progressive Relaxation:** Start from head to toe, focusing on each body part. Notice areas of tension or discomfort and explore their connection to stress triggers. Use progressive relaxation techniques to release muscular tension and promote relaxation responses.

  Tip: Schedule regular sessions for progressive relaxation to build familiarity and comfort with the practice.

  Example: Spend 10-15 minutes daily performing a progressive relaxation exercise, focusing on areas where tension accumulates, such as shoulders and neck.

- **Breath Awareness:** Use focused breathing exercises to cultivate present-moment awareness. Observe changes in breathing patterns during stressful situations to detect early signs of stress. Practice mindful breathing to regulate stress responses and promote emotional equilibrium.

  Tip: Practice mindful breathing during short breaks throughout the day to maintain emotional balance.

  Example: Practice deep breathing exercises for 5 minutes before stressful meetings or tasks to calm nerves and enhance focus.

- **Situational Mindfulness:** Apply mindfulness techniques during stressful interactions or tasks:

  - **Non-judgmental Observation:** Pause and observe thoughts, emotions, and bodily sensations without judgment. Acknowledge stress triggers and their influence on decision-making or performance. Practice non-judgmental observation to enhance emotional resilience and reduce reactivity.

    Tip: Use mindfulness reminders, such as a gentle alarm or sticky notes, to prompt moments of reflection during the day.

    Example: Reflect on your emotional response during a challenging conversation, noting how mindfulness helped you stay composed and focused.

  - **Stress Response Evaluation:** Reflect on habitual responses to stress. Identify reactive behaviours (e.g., avoidance, over-commitment) and explore alternative, mindful responses to mitigate stress impact. Develop adaptive coping strategies to manage stress triggers effectively.

Tip: Journal about your reactions to stress, exploring alternative responses that align with mindfulness principles.

Example: Evaluate how adopting a mindful approach to stress has influenced your ability to manage workload fluctuations and interpersonal challenges.

Feedback and Observational Assessment

360-Degree Feedback: Solicit feedback from peers, supervisors, and direct reports to gain diverse perspectives on stress triggers:

- **Behavioural Patterns:** Seek specific examples of behaviours or situations perceived as stressful. Compare self-perceptions with external observations to identify blind spots. Use feedback to refine self-awareness and recognize stress triggers from different perspectives.
  Tip: Schedule regular feedback sessions to maintain open communication and gather ongoing insights.
  Example: Request feedback on your stress management strategies from colleagues, incorporating their observations into your self-assessment.
- **Stress Impact Assessment:** Evaluate feedback to prioritize stress triggers requiring immediate attention. Collaborate with mentors or coaches to develop targeted stress management strategies. Utilize feedback to implement proactive measures and enhance stress resilience.
  Tip: Create action plans based on feedback to address identified stress triggers systematically.
  Example: Discuss feedback with a mentor to explore strategies for managing stress related to leadership responsibilities and team dynamics.
- **Behavioural Observation:** Engage in self-observation during stressful interactions:
  - **Behavioural Mapping:** Document changes in communication style, decision-making processes, or emotional responses under stress. Analyze deviations from typical behaviour to identify stress-induced patterns. Use

behavioural mapping to identify triggers and modify stress responses.

Tip: Use a structured format for behavioural mappings, such as a chart or diagram, to visualize patterns effectively.

Example: Review behavioural maps to identify patterns of over-commitment during periods of high workload, adjusting scheduling practices accordingly.

Utilize Stress Assessments and Personality Tests

Stress Assessments: Utilize validated tools (e.g., Perceived Stress Scale, Stress Audit) to quantify stress levels:

- **Stress Quantification:** Complete assessments regularly to track stress fluctuations and identify predominant stressors. Compare scores over time to assess stress management progress. Use quantitative data to prioritize stress management interventions effectively.

  Tip: Incorporate stress assessments into regular health check-ups or personal development plans.

  Example: Track stress levels using a validated scale, reviewing results quarterly to monitor progress in stress reduction efforts.

Personality Tests: Take personality assessments (e.g., Myers-Briggs Type Indicator, Big Five Personality Traits) to understand stress response tendencies:

- **Trait Analysis:** Identify personality traits (e.g., resilience, emotional stability) influencing stress perception and coping strategies. Tailor stress management approaches based on individual predispositions. Use personality insights to develop personalized stress management plans.

  Tip: Discuss personality test results with a therapist or counsellor to explore implications for stress management strategies.

  Example: Adapt stress management techniques based on personality insights, focusing on enhancing strengths and mitigating vulnerabilities.

Behavioral Analysis and Trigger Mapping

ABC Analysis: Apply the Antecedent-Behavior-Consequence model to analyze stress-triggering events:

- **Antecedents:** Identify triggers (e.g., deadlines, conflicts) preceding stress reactions. Document situational factors contributing to stress onset. Analyze environmental or interpersonal triggers that precede stress episodes.
  Tip: Use a structured approach to ABC analysis, outlining each component clearly for a thorough assessment.
  Example: Outline antecedents such as project deadlines and conflicting priorities that trigger stress reactions, exploring potential adjustments to mitigate their impact.
- **Behavioural Responses:** Document reactive behaviours (e.g., withdrawal, procrastination) triggered by stress. Assess the effectiveness of current coping strategies in managing stress outcomes. Develop alternative responses to minimize stress impact on behaviour and performance.
  Tip: Use behavioural journals to document changes in behaviour over time, identifying patterns related to stress triggers.
  Example: Reflect on how reactive behaviours impact productivity, experimenting with proactive strategies to promote resilience under stress.
- **Trigger Mapping:** Create visual representations of stress triggers encountered in professional settings:
  - **Visual Mapping:** Categorize triggers (e.g., workload, interpersonal dynamics) and annotate emotional and physiological responses. Use mapping to visualize stress patterns and facilitate strategic stress management planning. Identify recurring triggers and implement preventive measures to minimize stress.
    Tip: Update trigger maps regularly to reflect evolving stress triggers and mitigation strategies.

Example: Use a flowchart to map out stress triggers and corresponding coping strategies, adapting approaches based on observed effectiveness.

Case Studies Illustrating Effective Identification Methods

Case Study 6: Technology Firm's Stress Assessment Initiative

Overview: A technology firm implemented stress assessments to identify prevalent stressors among software developers.

Outcome: Analysis revealed coding deadlines and project scope changes as primary stress triggers. Tailored interventions included workload distribution improvements and stress resilience workshops. The firm experienced reduced absenteeism and increased productivity post-intervention.

Case Study 7: Healthcare Provider's Behavioral Mapping Project

Overview: A healthcare provider conducted behavioural mapping exercises among nursing staff to identify stressors in clinical settings.

Outcome: Mapping highlighted patient care demands and staff-patient communication challenges as significant stress triggers. Interventions included communication skills training and workload management strategies, resulting in improved staff morale and patient care outcomes.

Effective Stress Management Techniques

Overview of Proven Stress Management Strategies

Effective stress management involves a comprehensive approach to reducing the impact of stressors on mental and physical well-being. These strategies are essential for fostering resilience and maintaining a healthy work-life balance in professional environments.

Cognitive Behavioral Techniques (CBT)

Cognitive Behavioral Therapy (CBT) is a structured therapeutic approach that helps individuals identify and change negative thought patterns and behaviors contributing to stress. By challenging irrational beliefs and replacing them with rational alternatives, CBT enhances coping skills and significantly reduces stress levels.

Example and Guidance:

- **Scenario**: An individual tends to catastrophize about upcoming deadlines.
- **CBT Application**: Recognize the pattern of thinking the worst will happen, challenge this belief by examining past outcomes and the actual impact of deadlines, and develop more realistic expectations and coping strategies.
- **Guidance**: Keep a journal to track irrational thoughts and practice replacing them with rational responses.
- **Data Point**: A study by Hofmann et al. (2012) found that CBT significantly reduces symptoms of anxiety and stress, with effects lasting up to one year post-treatment.

Reader Actions:

1. **Start a Thought Journal**: Document negative thoughts and their triggers.
2. **Challenge Negative Beliefs**: Replace irrational thoughts with evidence-based, rational ones.

3. **Practice Regularly**: Consistency is key to seeing long-term benefits from CBT.

Considerations:

- **Personal Commitment**: CBT requires dedication and regular practice to be effective.
- **Professional Guidance**: Working with a trained therapist can enhance the effectiveness of CBT practices.

Mindfulness-Based Stress Reduction (MBSR)

Mindfulness-Based Stress Reduction (MBSR) incorporates mindfulness practices like meditation, body scans, and mindful movement to increase awareness of present-moment experiences without judgment. It helps individuals observe stress triggers objectively, reducing emotional reactivity and promoting overall well-being.

Example and Guidance:

- **Practice**: Focus on the sensation of breathing during stressful meetings or tasks.
- **Guidance**: Take a few minutes to close your eyes, breathe deeply, and observe thoughts and feelings without reacting to them. Use guided meditation apps like Headspace or Calm for daily practice.
- **Data Point**: A meta-analysis by Khoury et al. (2015) showed that MBSR significantly reduces stress, anxiety, and depression, with long-lasting effects.

Reader Actions:

1. **Daily Meditation**: Dedicate 10-15 minutes daily to mindfulness meditation.
2. **Mindful Breaks**: Integrate short mindfulness exercises into your workday.
3. **Use Apps**: Utilize apps like Insight Timer for guided sessions.

Considerations:

- **Initial Learning Curve**: Mindfulness practices may feel challenging initially but become easier with regular practice.
- **Environment**: Find a quiet space for practice to minimize distractions.

Relaxation Techniques

Various relaxation techniques, including progressive muscle relaxation, deep breathing exercises (diaphragmatic breathing), guided imagery, and meditation, help reduce muscle tension, lower heart rate, and promote relaxation responses.

Example and Guidance:

- **Practice**: Use progressive muscle relaxation before bed to unwind.
- **Guidance**: Start by tensing and then releasing each muscle group from head to toe, focusing on the sensations of relaxation with each release. Try apps like Insight Timer for guided relaxation sessions.
- **Data Point**: A study by Conrad & Roth (2007) found that progressive muscle relaxation significantly reduces stress and improves sleep quality.

Reader Actions:

1. **Set a Routine**: Practice relaxation techniques at the same time daily.
2. **Combine Techniques**: Use multiple methods (e.g., deep breathing with guided imagery) for enhanced effect.
3. **Track Progress**: Keep a journal of your relaxation practice and its impact on your stress levels.

Considerations:

- **Consistency**: Regular practice enhances the effectiveness of relaxation techniques.
- **Personal Preference**: Experiment with different techniques to find what works best for you.

Physical Activity

Regular exercise, such as walking, jogging, yoga, or dancing, releases endorphins and reduces stress hormones like cortisol. Physical activity improves mood, enhances sleep quality, and provides a healthy outlet for stress.

Example and Guidance:

- **Practice**: Incorporate physical activity into your daily routine by taking short breaks to stretch or go for a brisk walk.
- **Guidance**: Aim for at least 30 minutes of moderate exercise most days of the week for optimal stress relief. Join group fitness classes or find an exercise buddy to stay motivated.
- **Data Point**: The Anxiety and Depression Association of America (ADAA) states that regular physical activity reduces anxiety and depression, and improves overall mood.

Reader Actions:

1. **Schedule Workouts**: Plan exercise sessions into your daily calendar.
2. **Variety**: Mix different types of physical activities to keep it interesting.
3. **Set Goals**: Use fitness trackers to set and achieve exercise goals.

Considerations:

- **Time Management**: Finding time for exercise can be challenging but is crucial for stress management.
- **Enjoyment**: Choose activities you enjoy to stay motivated.

Balanced Diet

A nutritious diet supports overall well-being and resilience against stress. Avoid excessive caffeine and sugar intake, which can exacerbate stress levels and disrupt sleep patterns. Opt for a balanced diet rich in fruits, vegetables, lean proteins, and whole grains.

Example and Guidance:

- **Practice**: Plan meals ahead to ensure balanced nutrition throughout the day.

- **Guidance**: Include foods high in omega-3 fatty acids (e.g., salmon, walnuts) and antioxidants (e.g., berries, leafy greens) to support brain health and stress management. Use meal prep services or apps to simplify planning.
- **Data Point**: A study published in the "Journal of Nutrition & Food Sciences" found that a balanced diet reduces cortisol levels and improves mood.

Reader Actions:

1. **Meal Planning**: Plan weekly meals to ensure a balanced diet.
2. **Healthy Snacks**: Keep healthy snacks accessible to avoid junk food.
3. **Hydration**: Drink plenty of water to stay hydrated and support overall health.

Considerations:

- **Dietary Restrictions**: Tailor your diet to any specific health needs or restrictions.
- **Moderation**: Balance is key; avoid extreme diets that can cause additional stress.

Social Support

Cultivating strong relationships with friends, family, and colleagues provides emotional support and perspective during stressful times. Sharing experiences and receiving empathy enhances resilience and reduces feelings of isolation.

Example and Guidance:

- **Practice**: Schedule regular social activities or virtual meet-ups with supportive individuals.
- **Guidance**: Share concerns and seek advice or encouragement when facing work-related stressors. Join support groups or online communities for additional support.
- **Data Point**: Research by Holt-Lunstad et al. (2010) found that strong social connections improve longevity and reduce the impact of stress on health.

Reader Actions:

1. **Connect Regularly**: Schedule weekly catch-ups with friends or family.
2. **Join Groups**: Participate in social or hobby groups to expand your support network.
3. **Communicate Openly**: Share your feelings and seek support when needed.

Considerations:

- **Quality Over Quantity**: Focus on building meaningful relationships rather than numerous acquaintances.
- **Balance**: Ensure social activities do not become another source of stress.

Disconnect and Unplug

Manage digital device use and set boundaries for social media and screen time to prevent information overload and reduce stress. Prioritize face-to-face interactions and meaningful connections for deeper emotional support.

Example and Guidance:

- **Practice**: Designate tech-free zones or times during the day, such as during meals or before bedtime, to disconnect and unwind.
- **Guidance**: Use this time for relaxation activities or engaging in hobbies that promote stress relief. Apps like Moment can help track and reduce screen time.
- **Data Point**: A study by the American Psychological Association (APA) found that constant checking of devices increases stress levels, commonly known as "techno-stress."

Reader Actions:

1. **Set Boundaries**: Define specific times to disconnect from devices.
2. **Alternative Activities**: Engage in offline hobbies or relaxation techniques during unplugged times.
3. **Monitor Usage**: Use apps to track and manage your screen time effectively.

Considerations:

- **Initial Difficulty**: Adjusting to reduced screen time may be challenging initially but beneficial in the long run.
- **Digital Detox**: Periodic complete breaks from digital devices can be particularly refreshing.

Practical Tips for Immediate Stress Relief

In addition to long-term strategies, implementing immediate relief techniques can alleviate acute stress symptoms and restore emotional equilibrium quickly:

- **Deep Breathing Exercises**: Practice diaphragmatic breathing by inhaling deeply through the nose, holding for a count, and exhaling slowly through the mouth. Repeat several times to calm the nervous system and reduce stress.
- **Physical Activity Breaks**: Incorporate short bursts of physical activity, such as stretching or walking, to release tension and boost energy levels during stressful moments.
- **Social Connection**: Reach out to a trusted friend, family member, or colleague for support. A supportive conversation or simple check-in can provide perspective and reduce feelings of isolation.
- **Mindful Breaks**: Take brief breaks throughout the day to practice mindfulness or engage in activities that promote relaxation, such as listening to calming music or practicing deep breathing exercises.

Long-term Approaches for Sustainable Stress Reduction

Building resilience to stress involves adopting habits and strategies that support long-term well-being and prevent burnout:

- **Proper Sleep**: Establish a consistent sleep schedule and create a relaxing bedtime routine to improve sleep quality. Aim for 7-9 hours of uninterrupted sleep each night to support cognitive function and emotional resilience.

- **Healthy Lifestyle Habits**: Maintain a balanced diet, stay hydrated, and avoid excessive alcohol and caffeine consumption. Nutritious meals and regular hydration support physical health and enhance stress management capabilities.
- **Hobbies and Relaxation Activities**: Engage in hobbies like painting, reading, gardening, or listening to music to unwind and recharge outside of work responsibilities. Hobbies provide a creative outlet and promote relaxation.
- **Professional Support**: Seek guidance from a therapist or counselor for personalized strategies to manage stress effectively. Professional support offers coping techniques, behavioral strategies, and emotional support tailored to individual needs.

Tips and Guidance

- **Set Realistic Goals**: Break down tasks into manageable steps to reduce overwhelm and enhance productivity. Set SMART (Specific, Measurable, Achievable, Relevant, Time-bound) goals to track progress effectively.
- **Practice Self-Compassion**: Be kind to yourself during stressful periods and acknowledge your efforts. Practice self-care activities that promote mental and emotional well-being, such as journaling or practicing gratitude.
- **Establish Boundaries**: Create clear boundaries between work and personal life to prevent burnout and maintain overall well-being. Schedule time for relaxation, hobbies, and social activities to recharge and rejuvenate.
- **Seek Professional Help When Needed**: Consult with a therapist or counselor for personalized guidance on stress management techniques. Professional support offers valuable insights and strategies for coping with stress effectively.

Conclusion

By integrating these effective stress management techniques into daily routines, individuals can mitigate the impact of stressors, enhance resilience, and promote overall well-being in professional settings. Recognizing the importance of proactive stress management fosters a healthier work environment and supports long-term career success.

Section 05

Promoting Work-Life Balance

Importance of Work-Life Balance for Mental Health

Work-life balance is not just a buzzword but a critical component of maintaining mental health, enhancing productivity, and fostering overall well-being. In today's fast-paced professional environments, achieving a healthy equilibrium between work responsibilities and personal life commitments is paramount to prevent burnout and sustain long-term career satisfaction.

Mental Health Impact: Research consistently highlights the detrimental effects of prolonged work stress on mental health. Individuals experiencing high levels of work-life conflict often report symptoms of anxiety, depression, and dissatisfaction with their jobs. Prioritizing work-life balance supports mental resilience, reduces stress levels, and promotes emotional well-being, ultimately leading to greater job satisfaction and improved overall happiness.

Example and Guidance: Studies show that companies with supportive work-life balance policies experience higher employee retention rates and lower absenteeism. For instance, companies like Patagonia and Microsoft have implemented flexible work schedules and comprehensive wellness programs, resulting in improved employee well-being and organizational success.

Productivity and Creativity: Maintaining a balanced lifestyle not only benefits mental health but also enhances cognitive function and creativity. Taking breaks and engaging in leisure activities rejuvenates the mind, boosts motivation, and improves problem-solving skills. Employees who have the opportunity to recharge outside of work are more likely to bring fresh perspectives and innovative ideas to their jobs, leading to increased productivity and creativity.

Example and Guidance: Google's "20% Time" policy allows employees to spend a portion of their workweek on projects of personal interest. This initiative has led to the development of new products and technologies, demonstrating how work-life balance can foster creativity and drive organizational innovation.

Strategies to Achieve and Maintain Balance

Achieving work-life balance requires deliberate strategies to manage time effectively, set boundaries, and prioritize personal well-being alongside professional responsibilities.

- **Setting Boundaries:** Establishing clear boundaries between work and personal life is essential to prevent work from encroaching on personal time. Communicate expectations with colleagues and supervisors regarding availability outside of work hours to maintain a healthy separation and reduce stress.

  Example and Guidance: Consider implementing a "no-emails after work hours" policy or setting specific times for uninterrupted personal activities. This approach helps employees disconnect from work-related responsibilities and focus on rejuvenation and family time.

- **Time Management:** Effective time management is key to balancing work demands and personal life commitments. Utilize techniques such as prioritizing tasks, creating schedules, and using productivity tools to optimize work efficiency and minimize time spent on non-essential activities.

  Example and Guidance: Use time-blocking techniques to allocate dedicated time slots for different tasks, ensuring a balanced allocation of time between work responsibilities and personal interests. This method enhances productivity and reduces the stress associated with multitasking.

- **Flexibility and Adaptability:** Embrace flexible work arrangements, such as remote work options or flexible hours, to accommodate personal commitments and promote work-life integration. Flexible policies empower employees to manage work responsibilities while attending to personal needs, resulting in higher job satisfaction and improved work-life balance.

  Example and Guidance: Companies like IBM have successfully implemented remote work policies, allowing employees to work from home or other locations. This flexibility not only enhances employee morale but also reduces commuting stress and improves overall work-life harmony.

- **Self-Care Practices:** Incorporate regular self-care activities into daily routines to promote physical and mental well-being. Activities such as exercise, meditation, or engaging hobbies help alleviate stress, improve mood, and increase resilience against work-related pressures.

  Example and Guidance: Dedicate time each day for self-care practices, such as mindfulness meditation or yoga, to recharge and maintain emotional equilibrium. These practices not only enhance overall well-being but also improve focus and productivity during work hours.

- **Additional Strategies:**
    - **Set A Realistic Schedule:** Establish realistic deadlines and workload expectations to avoid overwhelm and maintain balance.
    - **Focus On Your Well-Being:** Prioritize your health and happiness as essential components of overall success.
    - **Say 'No':** Learn to decline tasks or commitments that exceed your capacity without guilt.
    - **Take Breaks:** Regularly step away from work to rest and recharge, improving focus and creativity.
    - **Create A Work-From-Home Routine:** Establish routines that delineate work and personal time when working remotely.
    - **Leave Work at Work:** Mentally and physically disengage from work when off-duty to prevent burnout.
    - **Exercise Your Options:** Explore different ways of working that suit your lifestyle and career aspirations.
    - **Work Smarter, Not Harder:** Focus on efficiency and effectiveness rather than simply increasing hours worked.
    - **The Importance of Self-Care:** Prioritize activities that promote physical, mental, and emotional well-being.

- Leveraging Flexibility in the Workplace: Utilize flexible work arrangements to optimize work-life integration.
- **Spend Time in Nature:** Reconnect with nature to reduce stress and improve overall well-being.

Conclusion

Prioritizing work-life balance is essential for maintaining mental health, enhancing job satisfaction, and achieving sustainable success in professional endeavors. By implementing proactive strategies, setting boundaries, and prioritizing personal well-being, individuals can cultivate a harmonious balance between work and life, leading to greater overall happiness and fulfillment. Achieving work-life balance is not just a personal goal but a strategic imperative for thriving in today's dynamic work environments.

Section 06

Mindfulness and Meditation Practices

Benefits of Mindfulness in Reducing Workplace Stress

Mindfulness practices offer a wealth of benefits that significantly reduce workplace stress and improve overall mental health. Here are some key advantages, supported by research and examples:

Reduced Rumination:

- **Research Insight**: Studies have shown that mindfulness can help break the cycle of negative thinking and over-analysis, which are common in stress and anxiety disorders. A study published in the *Journal of Clinical Psychology* found that mindfulness meditation significantly reduces rumination and stress.
- **Example**: Employees at Aetna who participated in a mindfulness program reported a 28% reduction in stress levels and a 20% improvement in sleep quality.
- **Guidance for Organizations**: Implement mindfulness programs that focus on reducing rumination to help employees break negative thought cycles.
- **Guidance for Individuals**: Practice mindfulness meditation to help reduce rumination and improve mental clarity.

Stress Reduction:

- **Research Insight**: Mindfulness meditation has been shown to reduce cortisol levels, a hormone associated with stress. A study by the University of Massachusetts Medical School found that participants in an 8-week mindfulness-based stress reduction (MBSR) program experienced significant reductions in perceived stress.
- **Example**: Intel's "Awake@Intel" mindfulness program led to a 2-point decrease in stress levels (on a 10-point scale) among participants.
- **Guidance for Organizations**: Offer MBSR programs to employees to help reduce overall stress levels.

- **Guidance for Individuals**: Participate in MBSR programs or practice mindfulness meditation regularly to manage stress.

Boosts to Working Memory:

- **Research Insight**: Mindfulness enhances working memory capacity. A study from the University of California, Santa Barbara, demonstrated that mindfulness training improved working memory and GRE reading comprehension scores.
- **Example**: Soldiers in the U.S. military who practiced mindfulness training showed improved working memory and cognitive performance under stress.
- **Guidance for Organizations**: Integrate mindfulness training into professional development programs to enhance cognitive performance.
- **Guidance for Individuals**: Engage in mindfulness exercises to improve memory and focus, especially during stressful periods.

Improved Focus:

- **Research Insight**: Mindfulness training increases attention span and concentration. Research from Harvard Medical School indicates that mindfulness meditation can increase the brain's capacity for attention.
- **Example**: At General Mills, employees who participated in a mindfulness program reported a 47% increase in their ability to focus and a 23% decrease in stress.
- **Guidance for Organizations**: Implement mindfulness programs to improve employee focus and productivity.
- **Guidance for Individuals**: Practice mindfulness techniques, such as focused breathing, to enhance concentration.

Less Emotional Reactivity:

- **Research Insight**: Mindfulness fosters emotional regulation, reducing impulsive reactions to stressful situations. A study published in *Emotion* found that mindfulness reduces emotional reactivity and increases emotional stability.

- **Example**: Google's mindfulness program, "Search Inside Yourself," has helped employees manage emotional reactivity, leading to better teamwork and communication.
- **Guidance for Organizations**: Provide mindfulness training to help employees manage emotional responses and improve teamwork.
- **Guidance for Individuals**: Use mindfulness practices to regulate emotions and respond more calmly to stress.

More Cognitive Flexibility:

- **Research Insight**: Practicing mindfulness enhances cognitive flexibility, enabling better problem-solving and adaptability. Research in the journal *Psychological Science* found that mindfulness training improves cognitive flexibility.
- **Example**: Participants in a mindfulness program at SAP reported increased creativity and flexibility in problem-solving.
- **Guidance for Organizations**: Encourage mindfulness practices to enhance problem-solving skills and adaptability among employees.
- **Guidance for Individuals**: Engage in mindfulness exercises to boost creativity and cognitive flexibility.

Relationship Satisfaction:

- **Research Insight**: Mindfulness improves communication and empathy, leading to more satisfying and supportive relationships. A study in the *Journal of Marital and Family Therapy* found that mindfulness is associated with greater relationship satisfaction and reduced relationship stress.
- **Example**: Mindfulness training at Ford Motor Company helped employees develop better interpersonal skills, improving workplace relationships and collaboration.
- **Guidance for Organizations**: Offer mindfulness programs to enhance interpersonal skills and improve workplace relationships.
- **Guidance for Individuals**: Practice mindfulness to foster empathy and improve communication in personal and professional relationships.

Enhanced Self-Insight, Morality, Intuition, and Fear Modulation:

- **Research Insight**: Mindfulness practices strengthen the middle prefrontal cortex, improving self-awareness, moral reasoning, intuitive thinking, and fear modulation. A study in the journal *Psychiatry Research: Neuroimaging* found that mindfulness meditation is associated with increased gray matter in brain regions involved in these functions.
- **Example**: Leaders at LinkedIn who engaged in mindfulness training reported enhanced self-insight and decision-making abilities.
- **Guidance for Organizations**: Encourage mindfulness training for leaders to enhance their decision-making and ethical reasoning.
- **Guidance for Individuals**: Engage in mindfulness practices to improve self-awareness and moral reasoning.

Reduced Anxiety:

- **Research Insight**: Mindfulness reduces symptoms of anxiety, providing a sense of calm and stability. A meta-analysis published in *JAMA Internal Medicine* found that mindfulness meditation programs can improve anxiety symptoms.
- **Example**: Mindfulness programs at Procter & Gamble have helped employees manage anxiety, resulting in lower absenteeism rates.
- **Guidance for Organizations**: Implement mindfulness programs to help employees manage anxiety and reduce absenteeism.
- **Guidance for Individuals**: Practice mindfulness meditation to reduce anxiety and enhance emotional stability.

Reduction of Implicit Age and Race Bias:

- **Research Insight**: Mindfulness meditation has been shown to reduce unconscious biases, fostering a more inclusive and equitable workplace. A study in the journal *Social Psychological and Personality Science* found that brief mindfulness meditation can reduce implicit bias.

- **Example**: Diversity training programs incorporating mindfulness at companies like Salesforce have led to more inclusive workplace cultures.
- **Guidance for Organizations**: Incorporate mindfulness into diversity training programs to reduce implicit biases.
- **Guidance for Individuals**: Practice mindfulness to become more aware of and reduce personal biases.

Prevention and Treatment of Depression:

- **Research Insight**: Mindfulness-Based Cognitive Therapy (MBCT) can prevent the recurrence of depression and alleviate depressive symptoms. A study in *The Lancet* found that MBCT is as effective as antidepressants in preventing depression relapse.
- **Example**: Mindfulness programs at Dow Chemical have been effective in reducing depressive symptoms among employees.
- **Guidance for Organizations**: Offer MBCT programs to support employees dealing with depression.
- **Guidance for Individuals**: Participate in MBCT programs or practice mindfulness to manage depression symptoms.

Increased Body Satisfaction:

- **Research Insight**: Mindfulness promotes a positive body image and acceptance. A study in the journal *Body Image* found that mindfulness is associated with higher body satisfaction.
- **Example**: Mindfulness initiatives at Unilever have improved body satisfaction and self-esteem among employees.
- **Guidance for Organizations**: Implement mindfulness programs to support positive body image and self-esteem among employees.
- **Guidance for Individuals**: Practice mindfulness to develop a more positive body image and self-acceptance.

Improved Cognition:

- **Research Insight**: Mindfulness enhances cognitive functions such as attention, memory, and executive functioning. A study in the journal *Mindfulness* found that mindfulness practice leads to improvements in cognitive performance.
- **Example**: Employees at Adobe who participated in mindfulness training reported better cognitive function and decision-making skills.
- **Guidance for Organizations**: Promote mindfulness training to enhance cognitive performance among employees.
- **Guidance for Individuals**: Engage in mindfulness exercises to improve attention, memory, and decision-making.

Reduced Distractions:

- **Research Insight**: Mindfulness meditation trains the brain to stay focused and reduce distractions. Research from the University of Wisconsin-Madison found that mindfulness meditation improves sustained attention.
- **Example**: Mindfulness programs at Microsoft have helped employees reduce distractions and improve productivity.
- **Guidance for Organizations**: Implement mindfulness programs to help employees stay focused and reduce workplace distractions.
- **Guidance for Individuals**: Practice mindfulness to improve focus and reduce distractions.

Empathy Enhancement:

- **Research Insight**: Regular mindfulness practice increases empathy and understanding in social interactions. A study in the journal *Psychological Science* found that mindfulness meditation promotes empathy and prosocial behavior.
- **Example**: Mindfulness training at Facebook has enhanced employees' empathy and collaboration.
- **Guidance for Organizations**: Encourage mindfulness training to foster empathy and collaboration among employees.

- **Guidance for Individuals**: Practice mindfulness to develop empathy and improve social interactions.

Health Benefits:

- **Research Insight**: Mindfulness meditation boosts immune function and overall physical health. A study in the *Annals of the New York Academy of Sciences* found that mindfulness meditation enhances immune response.
- **Example**: Health initiatives incorporating mindfulness at Google have led to improved physical health outcomes among employees.
- **Guidance for Organizations**: Include mindfulness in health and wellness programs to boost employee health.
- **Guidance for Individuals**: Engage in mindfulness practices to improve immune function and overall health.

Improved Sleep:

- **Research Insight**: Mindfulness helps manage sleep disorders and promotes restful sleep. A study in JAMA *Internal Medicine* found that mindfulness meditation improves sleep quality and reduces insomnia symptoms.
- **Example**: Mindfulness programs at Apple have helped employees improve their sleep quality and overall well-being.
- **Guidance for Organizations**: Implement mindfulness programs to help employees improve sleep quality.
- **Guidance for Individuals**: Practice mindfulness meditation to enhance sleep quality and manage insomnia.

Faster Information Processing:

- **Research Insight**: Mindfulness improves the speed at which the brain processes information. A study in the journal *Consciousness and Cognition* found that mindfulness meditation enhances information processing speed.

- **Example**: Employees at IBM who practiced mindfulness reported quicker decision-making and enhanced problem-solving abilities.
- **Guidance for Organizations**: Promote mindfulness training to improve information processing and decision-making among employees.
- **Guidance for Individuals**: Engage in mindfulness practices to enhance cognitive processing speed.

Decreased Distress Contagion:

- **Research Insight**: Mindfulness reduces the spread of distress in social situations. A study in the journal *Emotion* found that mindfulness reduces emotional contagion.
- **Example**: Mindfulness training at Twitter has helped employees manage their emotional responses and reduce workplace stress.
- **Guidance for Organizations**: Implement mindfulness programs to reduce emotional contagion and improve workplace dynamics.
- **Guidance for Individuals**: Practice mindfulness to manage emotional responses and reduce the impact of others' stress.

Constructive Response to Relationship Stress:

- **Research Insight**: Mindfulness enables constructive responses to relationship stress, reducing conflict and increasing empathy. A study in the journal *Psychoneuroendocrinology* found that mindfulness improves emotional regulation in relationships.
- **Example**: Mindfulness programs at Johnson & Johnson have enhanced employees' relationship skills, leading to better teamwork and communication.
- **Guidance for Organizations**: Offer mindfulness training to improve employees' relationship management skills.
- **Guidance for Individuals**: Engage in mindfulness practices to handle relationship stress more constructively.

Techniques for Incorporating Mindfulness into Daily Routines

Incorporating mindfulness into daily routines can significantly reduce stress and improve overall well-being. Here are some practical techniques:

Quick and Easy Meditation:

- **Find a Comfortable Position**: Sit on a straight-backed chair or cross-legged on the floor.
- **Focus on Breathing**: Concentrate on the sensations of air flowing into your nostrils and out of your mouth, or the rising and falling of your belly as you inhale and exhale.
- **Expand Your Focus**: After narrowing your focus on your breath, become aware of sounds, sensations, and thoughts. Embrace and consider each without judgment.
- **Return to Breathing**: If your mind starts to race, return your focus to your breathing. Gradually expand your awareness again.
- **Example**: A marketing executive at Amazon uses this technique during breaks to refresh and refocus, leading to increased productivity.

Open Awareness:

- **Choose a Routine Activity**: Select an activity like eating, walking, showering, cooking, or gardening.
- **Engage Your Senses**: Bring your attention to the physical and emotional sensations involved in the activity.
- **Practice Mindful Breathing**: Breathe in through your nose, allowing the air to fill your lungs, and exhale slowly through your mouth.
- **Single-Tasking**: Focus entirely on the task at hand, engaging each of your senses. Allow thoughts and emotions to come and go like clouds passing through the sky.
- **Refocus Attention**: If your mind wanders, gently bring your focus back to the current sensation.
- **Example**: A software developer at Microsoft practices mindful walking during lunch breaks, leading to reduced stress and better focus in the afternoon.

Body Scan:

- **Before Bed or Upon Waking**: Perform a body scan to relax and enhance mindfulness. Pay attention to each part of your body from head to toe, noticing any sensations without judgment.
- **Example**: A manager at Cisco uses a body scan meditation every morning to start the day with a clear and focused mind, resulting in better decision-making throughout the day.

Hand on Heart:

- **Quick Stress Relief**: Close your eyes, place your hand on your heart, and take deep breaths. Focus on the rising and falling of your chest and the beats of your heart.
- **Example**: Employees at American Express use the "hand on heart" technique before important meetings to reduce anxiety and improve focus.

Palm Reading:

- **Bring Presence**: Close your eyes, take a deep breath, and slowly trace the lines on your palm. Feel the touch of your fingertips on your palm, relaxing your shoulders.
- **Example**: Customer service representatives at Zappos use this technique to stay calm and present during challenging customer interactions.

Mindful Driving:

- **Stay Present**: While driving, pay attention to the sensations, sounds, and sights around you. Practice mindful breathing to stay calm and focused.
- **Example**: Delivery drivers at UPS practice mindful driving to reduce stress and stay alert on the road.

Guided Meditation Exercises for Stress Relief

Guided meditation exercises can provide structured mindfulness practice and enhance stress relief. Here are some effective techniques:

Progressive Relaxation:

- **Body Awareness**: Focus on tensing and then relaxing each muscle group in your body, starting from your toes and moving up to your head.
- **Example**: Employees at Coca-Cola use progressive relaxation techniques to unwind after high-pressure workdays.

Loving-Kindness Meditation:

- **Cultivate Compassion**: Focus on sending thoughts of love and kindness to yourself, loved ones, acquaintances, and even those with whom you have conflicts.
- **Example**: Participants in a mindfulness program at LinkedIn practice loving-kindness meditation to foster a more compassionate and supportive work environment.

Mindfulness of Emotions:

- **Emotional Awareness**: Observe your emotions without judgment, allowing them to come and go like waves in the ocean.
- **Example**: HR professionals at Accenture use mindfulness of emotions exercises to manage their own emotional responses and support employees effectively.

Examples and Case Studies

Integrating real-life examples and case studies can illustrate the effectiveness of mindfulness practices in workplace settings:

Case Study: Google's "20% Time":

- **Overview**: Google allows employees to spend 20% of their work time on projects they are passionate about, fostering creativity and reducing stress.
- **Outcome**: This policy has led to the creation of innovative products like Gmail and Google News.

Example: Patagonia's Flexibility:

- **Overview**: Patagonia offers flexible work schedules and outdoor breaks, promoting work-life balance and reducing employee stress.
- **Outcome**: This approach has resulted in higher job satisfaction and retention rates.

Case Study: SAP's Mindfulness Programs:

- **Overview**: SAP's comprehensive mindfulness programs have shown significant improvements in employee well-being, including reductions in stress levels, improved focus, and better overall health.

Tips for Incorporating Mindfulness into Daily Routines

Practice Mindful Breathing: Spend a few minutes each day focusing on your breath. This can be done anywhere and at any time to quickly reduce stress.

- **Example**: Set a timer for 5 minutes each morning to practice mindful breathing before starting your workday.

Engage in Mindful Walking: Take a walk and focus on the sensations of walking, the sounds around you, and your breath. This helps clear the mind and reduce stress.

- **Example**: Use your lunch break for a 10-minute mindful walk around your office or neighborhood.

Foster Mindful Communication: Practice active listening and speak with intention during conversations. This enhances relationships and reduces misunderstandings.

- **Example**: In meetings, focus on listening fully to colleagues without planning your response while they are speaking.

Take Mindful Breaks: Throughout the day, take short breaks to practice mindfulness. This can be as simple as a few minutes of deep breathing or a brief walk.

- **Example**: Schedule 5-minute mindfulness breaks every hour to stand, stretch, and practice deep breathing.

Conscious Perception of Nature: Spend time in nature, fully engaging your senses to appreciate the sights, sounds, and smells around you.

- **Example**: Take weekend trips to parks or natural reserves to disconnect from work and reconnect with nature.

Use Technology: Apps like Headspace and Calm offer guided meditations and mindfulness exercises that can easily be integrated into daily routines.

- **Example**: Download a mindfulness app and set reminders to meditate or practice mindfulness exercises daily.

Create a Mindful Workspace: Organize your workspace to reduce distractions and promote a sense of calm. Include elements like plants, personal items, and ergonomic furniture.

- **Example**: Add a small plant to your desk and declutter your workspace to create a more peaceful environment.

Incorporate Mindfulness into Meetings: Start meetings with a brief mindfulness exercise to help everyone focus and reduce stress.

- **Example**: Begin each team meeting with 2 minutes of guided breathing exercises to center and focus participants.

Mindfulness Reminders: Set reminders on your phone or computer to take mindfulness breaks throughout the day.

- **Example**: Set hourly reminders on your phone to pause and take three deep breaths.

To-Do List

1. **Practice Mindful Breathing**: Dedicate a few minutes daily to focus on your breath.
2. **Engage in Mindful Walking**: Take regular walks, focusing on the sensory experiences.
3. **Foster Mindful Communication**: Practice active listening and intentional speaking.
4. **Take Mindful Breaks**: Incorporate short mindfulness breaks throughout your day.
5. **Spend Time in Nature**: Regularly spend time outdoors, fully engaging your senses.
6. **Incorporate Guided Meditation**: Use guided meditation exercises like progressive relaxation or loving-kindness meditation.
7. **Set Realistic Schedules**: Create manageable schedules that balance work and personal time.
8. **Focus on Well-Being**: Prioritize activities that enhance your physical and mental health.
9. **Practice Saying 'No'**: Set boundaries by declining additional responsibilities that may cause stress.
10. **Create Work-From-Home Routines**: Establish clear routines if working from home to maintain work-life balance.
11. **Leave Work at Work**: Avoid bringing work-related tasks and stress into your personal time.
12. **Exercise Your Options**: Utilize flexible work arrangements if available.
13. **Work Smarter, Not Harder**: Focus on efficient work practices to reduce stress.
14. **Prioritize Tasks and Delegate**: Use tools like the Eisenhower Matrix to manage priorities and delegate tasks.

By incorporating these mindfulness and meditation practices into your daily routine, you can significantly reduce workplace stress, enhance mental health, and improve overall well-being. Recognizing the importance of proactive stress management fosters a healthier work environment and supports long-term career success.

Physical Health and Stress Reduction

Impact of Physical Activity on Stress Levels

Regular physical activity is a powerful tool for reducing stress and improving overall well-being. Exercise helps mitigate the negative effects of stress by reducing the body's stress hormones, such as adrenaline and cortisol, and stimulating the production of endorphins, chemicals in the brain that act as natural painkillers and mood elevators.

Statistics and Data:

- According to the American Psychological Association (APA), more than half of adults who exercise report feeling less stressed. Furthermore, the APA's Stress in America survey found that 53% of adults say they feel good about themselves after exercising, and 30% say they feel less stressed.
- A study published in the *Journal of Exercise Physiology* found that regular aerobic exercise can decrease overall levels of tension, elevate and stabilize mood, improve sleep, and enhance self-esteem. Even five minutes of aerobic exercise can stimulate anti-anxiety effects.

Recommendations for Integrating Exercise into the Workday

Integrating exercise into the workday doesn't require a significant time commitment. Small, consistent efforts can lead to substantial benefits. Here are some practical recommendations:

1. Micro-Workouts:

- Encourage employees to take short, frequent breaks to stretch or walk around. Even five to ten minutes of physical activity can refresh the mind and body.

- Desk exercises such as seated leg raises, chair squats, and shoulder rolls can be performed without leaving the workstation.

2. Walking Meetings:

- Replace traditional sit-down meetings with walking meetings. This not only adds physical activity but can also enhance creativity and productivity.

3. Office Exercise Programs:

- Implement office-wide exercise initiatives, such as yoga or Pilates classes during lunch breaks, or morning stretching sessions. Many companies offer incentives for participation to increase engagement.

4. Active Commuting:

- Encourage employees to walk or cycle to work if possible. For those who drive, suggest parking further from the office or getting off public transportation a stop early to incorporate more walking.

5. On-Site Fitness Facilities:

- If feasible, provide on-site fitness facilities or partner with local gyms to offer employees convenient access to exercise equipment and classes.

Ergonomic Tips for Reducing Physical Stress at Work

Creating an ergonomic workspace is crucial for reducing physical stress and preventing long-term injuries. Here are some ergonomic tips:

1. Proper Chair and Desk Setup:

- Ensure that chairs provide adequate support for the lower back. Adjust the height so feet rest flat on the floor, with knees at a 90-degree angle.

- Desks should be at a height where forearms are parallel to the floor when typing. Use adjustable desks if possible to allow for alternating between sitting and standing.

2. Monitor Placement:

- Position monitors at eye level, about an arm's length away. This reduces strain on the neck and eyes.

3. Keyboard and Mouse:

- Keep keyboards and mice close enough to prevent reaching. Wrists should be straight and elbows close to the body.

4. Regular Breaks:

- Follow the 20-20-20 rule: every 20 minutes, look at something 20 feet away for at least 20 seconds to reduce eye strain.

5. Workspace Layout:

- Arrange workspaces to minimize the need for repetitive movements and awkward postures. Ensure that frequently used items are within easy reach.

Guidance for Organizations

To effectively support the physical health of employees, organizations should take the following steps:

Immediate Actions:

- Conduct a survey to understand employees' current physical activity levels and interest in workplace exercise programs.
- Introduce short stretching or exercise breaks during meetings and throughout the workday.

Long-Term Strategies:

- Develop a comprehensive workplace wellness program that includes regular physical activities, ergonomic assessments, and educational sessions on the benefits of physical health.
- Partner with local gyms or fitness instructors to provide on-site or virtual exercise classes.

Considerations:

- Ensure inclusivity by offering a variety of activities that cater to different fitness levels and preferences.
- Provide flexible options for remote workers, such as virtual exercise sessions and tips for creating ergonomic home office setups.

Examples and Case Studies:

- **Google:** Google offers various wellness programs, including onsite fitness centers, group exercise classes, and ergonomic workstations, to promote employee health and reduce stress.
- **Microsoft:** Microsoft's "Health and Wellness" program includes fitness challenges, subsidized gym memberships, and ergonomic office setups to encourage physical activity and overall well-being.
- **Johnson & Johnson:** Their "Energy for Performance" program incorporates physical activity as a core component of employee well-being, offering resources such as fitness classes and wellness challenges.

Guidance for Individuals:

Employees can take proactive steps to integrate physical activity into their daily routine and advocate for ergonomic adjustments in their workspace:

1. Incorporate Movement into Your Day:

- Take short, frequent breaks to stand, stretch, and move around. Use a timer or reminder app to prompt you to move every hour.
- Choose activities that you enjoy, such as walking, cycling, or yoga, to make exercise a regular part of your routine.

2. Advocate for Ergonomic Improvements:

- Request ergonomic assessments and adjustments from your employer to ensure your workstation is set up correctly.
- Use ergonomic accessories such as wrist supports, footrests, and adjustable monitor stands to enhance your workspace.

3. Utilize Workplace Resources:

- Take advantage of any on-site fitness facilities, exercise classes, or wellness programs offered by your employer.
- Participate in workplace wellness challenges and initiatives to stay motivated and engaged.

4. Prioritize Self-Care:

- Make time for regular physical activity, even if it's just a short walk during your lunch break.
- Practice good posture and take regular breaks to avoid physical strain and fatigue.

Action Points for Implementing Physical Health Strategies

To effectively integrate these strategies into the workplace, consider the following action points:

Immediate Actions:

- Conduct a survey to understand employees' current physical activity levels and interest in workplace exercise programs.

- Introduce short stretching or exercise breaks during meetings and throughout the workday.

Long-Term Strategies:

- Develop a comprehensive workplace wellness program that includes regular physical activities, ergonomic assessments, and educational sessions on the benefits of physical health.
- Partner with local gyms or fitness instructors to provide on-site or virtual exercise classes.

Considerations:

- Ensure inclusivity by offering a variety of activities that cater to different fitness levels and preferences.
- Provide flexible options for remote workers, such as virtual exercise sessions and tips for creating ergonomic home office setups.

Examples and Case Studies:

- **Google:** Google offers various wellness programs, including onsite fitness centers, group exercise classes, and ergonomic workstations, to promote employee health and reduce stress.
- **Microsoft:** Microsoft's "Health and Wellness" program includes fitness challenges, subsidized gym memberships, and ergonomic office setups to encourage physical activity and overall well-being.
- **Johnson & Johnson:** Their "Energy for Performance" program incorporates physical activity as a core component of employee well-being, offering resources such as fitness classes and wellness challenges.

Conclusion and Call to Action

Physical health is an integral part of managing stress and maintaining overall well-being. By incorporating regular exercise and ergonomic practices into the workday, employees can experience reduced stress levels, improved mood, and enhanced productivity.

Call to Action:

- Employers: Invest in creating a supportive environment that promotes physical activity and ergonomic practices.
- Employees: Take proactive steps to integrate physical activity into your daily routine and advocate for ergonomic adjustments in your workspace.

By prioritizing physical health, we can create a healthier, happier, and more productive work environment.

<h1 align="center">Section 08</h1>

<h1 align="center">Effective Communication and Conflict Resolution</h1>

Organizational Strategies

Importance of Clear Communication in Stress Management

Statistics and Studies: Effective communication is crucial for managing workplace stress. According to the American Psychological Association, 61% of employees cite communication issues as a primary source of stress. Organizations that prioritize clear communication channels report significant benefits, including a 23% reduction in stress levels and a 17% increase in job satisfaction (*Journal of Occupational Health Psychology*). Moreover, a study by the *International Journal of Business Communication* found that companies with strong communication strategies are 50% more likely to have lower employee turnover rates.

Examples and Insights:

- **Technology Startup**: In a technology startup, consistent and clear communication from leadership about project goals, timelines, and individual roles helped reduce employee anxiety and ensure alignment. For instance, during a software development phase, regular updates and transparent communication about challenges and progress eased tensions and fostered team cohesion.
- **Company Reorganization**: In contrast, a lack of communication during a company reorganization led to confusion, anxiety, and decreased morale among employees.

Reader Action: To promote clear communication within the organization:

1. **Implement Regular Updates**: Schedule frequent updates through team meetings, emails, and digital platforms to keep everyone informed about project developments and organizational changes.

2. **Encourage Two-Way Communication**: Create a culture where employees feel comfortable asking questions, providing feedback, and sharing concerns without fear of repercussions.

Tips:

- **Use Multiple Communication Channels**: Utilize a variety of channels such as face-to-face meetings, emails, instant messaging, and project management tools to ensure information reaches all employees effectively.
- **Provide Communication Training**: Offer workshops and seminars to enhance communication skills across different levels of the organization, focusing on active listening, clarity in communication, and empathy.

Considerations:

- **Tailor Communication Styles**: Recognize diverse communication preferences among team members and adapt your approach accordingly to foster understanding and engagement.
- **Feedback Loop**: Establish a feedback mechanism to assess the effectiveness of communication strategies and make adjustments based on employee input.

Individual Strategies

Effective Communication Skills for Individuals

Effective communication skills are essential for personal and professional success, enabling individuals to convey ideas clearly, build relationships, and navigate challenging situations.

Strategies:

- **Active Listening**: Practice active listening by focusing on the speaker, asking clarifying questions, and summarizing key points to demonstrate understanding.
- **Clarity and Conciseness**: Communicate thoughts and information clearly and concisely to avoid confusion and misinterpretation.

- **Assertiveness**: Express thoughts, opinions, and concerns confidently and respectfully, while also being receptive to others' viewpoints.
- **Empathy**: Demonstrate empathy by understanding and acknowledging others' emotions, perspectives, and experiences.
- **Constructive Feedback**: Provide feedback constructively, focusing on specific behaviors or actions rather than personal attributes, to promote growth and development.

Reader Action:

1. **Practice Active Listening**: Make a conscious effort to fully engage in conversations, minimizing distractions.
2. **Communicate Clearly**: Work on expressing your ideas clearly and concisely to avoid misunderstandings.
3. **Be Assertive**: Practice being assertive in your communications, ensuring your voice is heard while respecting others.

Tips:

- **Non-Verbal Cues**: Pay attention to body language, facial expressions, and tone of voice to enhance understanding.
- **Seek Feedback**: Regularly ask for feedback on your communication style to identify areas for improvement.

Considerations:

- **Cultural Sensitivity**: Be aware of cultural differences that may affect communication styles and preferences.
- **Adaptability**: Be flexible and willing to adapt your communication style to different situations and audiences.

Conflict Resolution Skills for Individuals

Conflict resolution skills enable individuals to address disagreements and disputes effectively, fostering collaboration and maintaining positive relationships.

Steps:

1. **Recognize and Acknowledge**: Acknowledge the presence of conflict and its impact on individuals and team dynamics.
2. **Remain Calm**: Manage emotions and approach the situation with composure and professionalism.
3. **Listen Actively**: Listen actively to understand the concerns and perspectives of all parties involved in the conflict.
4. **Seek Common Ground**: Identify shared goals and interests to facilitate collaborative problem-solving.
5. **Propose Solutions**: Brainstorm potential solutions together and select an option that addresses the underlying issues effectively.
6. **Follow Through**: Implement the agreed-upon solution and monitor its effectiveness, making adjustments as necessary to maintain positive outcomes.

Reader Action:

1. **Acknowledge Conflict**: Do not avoid conflicts; address them promptly and professionally.
2. **Practice Active Listening**: Ensure all parties feel heard and understood.
3. **Collaborate on Solutions**: Work together to find mutually acceptable solutions to conflicts.

Tips:

- **Stay Objective**: Focus on the issue, not the person, to maintain a professional approach.
- **Follow Up**: After resolving a conflict, check in with all parties to ensure the solution is working and to address any new concerns.

Considerations:

- **Emotional Intelligence**: Develop emotional intelligence to better manage your own emotions and understand those of others during conflicts.
- **Patience**: Be patient and give conflicts the time needed to be resolved effectively.

Building Supportive Relationships and Teamwork

Benefits of Supportive Relationships: Research from the *Journal of Applied Psychology* shows that strong workplace relationships and teamwork lead to lower stress levels, higher job satisfaction, and increased productivity. Teams that communicate well and support each other tend to perform better and exhibit greater resilience to stress.

Examples:

- **Healthcare Setting**: Regular team-building activities and open communication channels in a healthcare setting led to improved patient care outcomes and reduced stress among staff.
- **Retail Company**: A retail company improved interdepartmental collaboration and conflict resolution by fostering cross-functional team meetings and shared project goals, resulting in a 15% increase in overall sales performance.

Reader Action: To foster supportive relationships and teamwork:

1. **Organize Team-Building Activities**: Plan activities that encourage collaboration, trust-building, and camaraderie among team members.
2. **Promote Psychological Safety**: Create an environment where team members feel safe to share ideas, take risks, and express concerns without fear of judgment.
3. **Encourage Cross-Functional Collaboration**: Facilitate meetings and initiatives that involve multiple departments to promote understanding and cooperation.

Tips:

- **Recognition and Appreciation**: Acknowledge and celebrate team achievements and individual contributions to reinforce a supportive culture.
- **Effective Communication**: Maintain open lines of communication to ensure clarity, alignment on goals, and timely resolution of conflicts.
- **Conflict Resolution Skills**: Equip team members with conflict resolution training to address differences constructively and maintain positive relationships.

Considerations:

- **Leadership Role**: Leaders play a crucial role in fostering a supportive environment by modeling positive behaviors, encouraging collaboration, and addressing conflicts proactively.
- **Team Dynamics**: Understand and respect diverse perspectives and working styles within the team to leverage strengths and enhance teamwork effectiveness.

Data and Statistics

Communication and Stress:

- According to a study published in the *Journal of Applied Communication Research*, clear and transparent communication reduces workplace stress by 30%.
- The *International Journal of Business Communication* found that organizations with robust communication strategies experience 50% lower turnover rates.

Conflict Resolution:

- The *International Journal of Conflict Management* reports that effective conflict resolution strategies can decrease workplace tensions by 25% and increase team performance by 18%.

Supportive Relationships:

- A study by *Harvard Business Review* found that employees with strong workplace relationships are 70% less likely to experience burnout.

Insights and Enhanced Guidance

For Organizations:

- **Implement Feedback Systems**: Develop formal feedback systems where employees can share their thoughts on communication and conflict resolution practices.
- **Regular Training Sessions**: Schedule ongoing training sessions for employees to continuously improve their communication and conflict resolution skills.
- **Promote Open Communication**: Encourage an open-door policy where employees feel comfortable discussing issues with their supervisors.

For Individuals:

- **Practice Active Listening**: Engage fully in conversations, minimizing distractions.
- **Communicate Clearly**: Work on expressing ideas clearly and concisely.
- **Be Assertive**: Ensure your voice is heard while respecting others.
- **Acknowledge Conflict**: Address conflicts promptly and professionally.
- **Practice Empathy**: Understand and acknowledge others' emotions and perspectives.

Considerations:

- **Cultural Sensitivity**: Tailor communication and conflict resolution approaches to respect cultural differences within the team.
- **Ongoing Evaluation**: Regularly assess the effectiveness of communication and conflict resolution strategies and make necessary adjustments based on feedback.

Tips:

- **Use Technology**: Leverage tools like Slack, Microsoft Teams, and Asana to facilitate communication and project management.

- **Empathy Mapping**: Use empathy mapping exercises to understand team members' perspectives and improve communication strategies.

Notes:

- **Leadership Involvement**: Ensure that leaders are actively involved in communication and conflict resolution training to set a positive example.
- **Balance**: Strive to maintain a balance between professional and personal communication to foster a supportive work environment.

Action Points:

1. **Implement Regular Updates**: Keep everyone informed about project developments and organizational changes.
2. **Encourage Two-Way Communication**: Create a culture where employees feel comfortable sharing concerns without fear of repercussions.
3. **Provide Communication Training**: Enhance communication skills across different levels of the organization.
4. **Develop Feedback Systems**: Allow employees to share their thoughts on communication and conflict resolution practices.
5. **Organize Team-Building Activities**: Encourage collaboration and trust-building.
6. **Promote Psychological Safety**: Create an environment where team members feel safe to share ideas.
7. **Equip Team Members with Conflict Resolution Skills**: Address differences constructively and maintain positive relationships.

By incorporating these detailed insights, strategies, and examples, this chapter provides a comprehensive guide to effective communication and conflict resolution. It offers practical tools and techniques for both organizations and individuals to reduce stress and enhance overall workplace well-being. Recognizing the importance of clear communication and conflict resolution fosters a healthier work environment and supports long-term career success.

Leadership's Role in Stress Management

Understanding the Impact of Leadership on Mental Health

Leadership plays a crucial role in the mental health and well-being of employees. The way leaders interact with and support their staff profoundly affects their well-being, potentially making the difference between a productive, motivated workforce and one that is disengaged and apathetic. Effective leadership reduces workplace stress, improves morale and engagement, and builds trust within the workplace. Here are some key points supported by the latest research:

Impact on Stress Reduction:

- **Research Insight**: A study by the American Psychological Association (APA) found that 75% of employees reported that their direct manager plays a significant role in their stress levels. Leaders who provide clear direction, maintain open communication channels, and create a respectful and inclusive environment help reduce stress significantly.
- **Data Point**: The APA's 2021 Work and Well-Being Survey showed that employees with supportive managers reported 30% lower stress levels and 25% higher job satisfaction.

Employee Engagement:

- **Research Insight**: Gallup's State of the American Workplace report revealed that employees who feel their managers are invested in their well-being are 21% more engaged at work.
- **Data Point**: Gallup's 2022 report indicated that highly engaged teams show 41% lower absenteeism, 17% higher productivity, and 10% higher customer ratings.

Trust and Productivity:

- **Research Insight**: According to a study published in the *Harvard Business Review*, employees who trust their leaders report 74% less stress, 106% more energy at work, and 50% higher productivity.
- **Data Point**: The 2020 HBR study further highlighted that trust in leadership leads to a 29% increase in overall employee well-being.

Mental Health and Productivity:

- **Research Insight**: The World Health Organization (WHO) estimates that depression and anxiety cost the global economy $1 trillion per year in lost productivity. Leaders who prioritize mental health can mitigate these costs.
- **Data Point**: WHO's 2021 update reported that for every $1 invested in mental health interventions, there is a $4 return in improved health and productivity.

Guidance for Leaders

Leaders who understand their role in promoting mental health can provide clear direction, open communication channels so that employees feel safe to speak up, and ensure they are creating a healthy working environment where everyone feels respected and valued. They should also be mindful of task allocation to prevent overload and ensure regular feedback is given to make employees feel valued and informed about their performance. Moreover, leaders must take responsibility for their own well-being as acting as role models is essential. If a leader appears stressed or overwhelmed, there is usually a ripple effect across the whole organization, potentially impacting employee morale long-term. It is vital for leaders to develop healthy strategies for dealing with stress, such as mindfulness or meditation techniques, which will inspire others within the organization to do the same.

Identifying Signs of Poor Mental Health in Employees

Employee mental health is an integral part of workplace productivity and morale. As a leader, you have the opportunity to identify signs of poor mental health in your team and take proactive measures to ensure their well-being. It can be challenging to recognize when someone is struggling with their mental health, but there are some signs to watch for:

- **Lack of Motivation and Enthusiasm**: A noticeable decline in interest or excitement about work tasks or activities can indicate mental health struggles.
- **Low Energy Levels**: Increased fatigue, frequent breaks, or a general lack of energy during work hours may suggest underlying issues.
- **Changes in Behavior**: Significant changes in behavior, such as withdrawal from social interactions or increased irritability, can be warning signs.
- **Poor Performance**: A decline in work quality, increased mistakes, or missed deadlines may indicate that an employee is struggling.

Guidance for Leaders: By paying attention to these signs, leaders can take proactive measures such as offering counseling services or flexible working arrangements to support their employees' well-being. Providing access to counseling services or offering flexible working arrangements can demonstrate that you value your employees' well-being and are committed to maintaining a healthy work environment.

Strategies for Creating a Supportive Work Environment

Creating a supportive work environment is essential for promoting employee well-being. Here are some strategies that leaders can implement:

Open Communication:

- **Action**: Schedule regular one-on-one meetings with team members to discuss their workload and any concerns they might have.
- **Consideration**: Use these meetings not just to talk about work but also to understand their personal challenges and stressors.

Workload Management:

- **Action**: Implement a system for tracking workloads and redistribute tasks when necessary.

- **Tip**: Use project management tools like Asana or Trello to monitor workloads.

Recognition and Feedback:

- **Action**: Implement a regular feedback loop where employees can receive constructive criticism and praise.
- **Tip**: Use the "Start, Stop, Continue" method for feedback to provide balanced and actionable insights.

Flexible Working Arrangements:

- **Action**: Develop a flexible working policy that allows employees to adjust their schedules to meet personal needs.
- **Consideration**: Ensure that remote employees have access to the same resources and support as in-office employees.

Promote Work-Life Balance:

- **Action**: Encourage employees to take their full lunch breaks and to use their vacation days.
- **Tip**: Lead by example by taking your own breaks and vacations to show that it's acceptable and important.

Case Studies and Examples

Google:

- **Initiative**: Google has long been recognized for its comprehensive employee well-being programs, which include on-site wellness centers, mental health resources, and flexible work options.
- **Outcome**: Their holistic approach has led to high employee satisfaction and retention rates. For instance, Google's "Search Inside Yourself" program focuses on mindfulness and emotional intelligence, helping employees manage stress effectively.

Microsoft:

- **Initiative**: Microsoft introduced extensive mental health benefits and regular training for managers on recognizing and supporting mental health needs.
- **Outcome**: Their "Headspace for Work" initiative provides employees with access to meditation and mindfulness resources, significantly reducing stress levels across the organization.

Salesforce:

- **Initiative**: Salesforce emphasizes mental health through initiatives like "B-Well Together," a series of mental health and wellness sessions led by experts.
- **Outcome**: Their "Mindfulness Zones" in offices offer employees a quiet space to meditate and recharge, contributing to a more supportive work environment.

Intel:

- **Initiative**: Intel's "Employee Assistance Program" (EAP) provides confidential counseling services to employees and their families.
- **Outcome**: This program also includes stress management workshops, financial advice, and legal support, showcasing a holistic approach to employee well-being.

Training and Development Opportunities

Investing in leadership training and development is crucial for stress management. Here are some recommended programs and workshops:

Mindfulness and Stress Management Workshops:

- **Example**: Aetna's mindfulness program resulted in a 28% reduction in stress levels among participating employees.

Leadership Development Programs:

- **Example**: Dale Carnegie's Leadership Training for Managers has been shown to improve leadership effectiveness by 23% on average.

Mental Health First Aid Training:

- **Example**: The Mental Health First Aid program has trained over 2.6 million people worldwide, helping organizations better support employees with mental health issues.

Action Points for Leaders

To effectively manage stress within their teams, leaders should consider the following actions:

Immediate Actions:

- Conduct regular one-on-one meetings to check in on employees' well-being.
- Implement flexible work policies.
- Provide access to mental health resources, such as Employee Assistance Programs (EAPs).

Long-Term Strategies:

- Foster a culture of openness and support regarding mental health.
- Continuously invest in leadership training and development.
- Regularly review and adjust workplace policies to ensure they support employee well-being.

Insights and Tips

Consideration for Remote Employees:

- **Tip**: Use video conferencing tools to maintain personal connections with remote employees.

Role Modeling:

- **Action**: Share your own stress management practices with your team.

Feedback Loops:

- **Tip**: Use anonymous surveys to gather honest feedback.

Professional Support:

- **Consideration**: Partner with local mental health organizations to provide additional support and resources.

Conclusion

Leadership has a profound impact on employee well-being and stress management. By understanding their role, recognizing signs of poor mental health, creating a supportive work environment, and investing in their development, leaders can significantly improve their teams' mental health and productivity. Leaders who prioritize mental health and model effective stress management techniques set a positive example and create a healthier, more productive workplace.

Section 10

Building Resilience and Adaptability

Importance of Resilience and Adaptability in the Workplace

Resilience and adaptability are critical traits for success in today's fast-paced and ever-changing work environment. Here are some advanced statistics and data points that highlight their importance:

- **Impact on Productivity**: According to a study by the American Psychological Association (APA), resilient employees are 31% more productive than their less resilient counterparts. Resilience helps employees recover quickly from setbacks and maintain high levels of performance.
- **Employee Retention**: A survey by Deloitte found that 70% of resilient employees are more likely to stay with their current employer, compared to 43% of non-resilient employees. This indicates that resilience is a key factor in reducing turnover and retaining top talent.
- **Mental Health and Well-being**: The World Health Organization (WHO) reports that resilience can reduce the risk of depression and anxiety by up to 30%. Resilient individuals are better equipped to handle stress and maintain their mental health.
- **Organizational Success**: A study by McKinsey & Company found that companies with high levels of employee resilience and adaptability were 20% more likely to report strong financial performance.
- **Adaptability and Innovation**: According to a study by PwC, organizations that foster adaptability are 24% more likely to report significant innovation and market leadership.

Insights: The ability to adapt quickly and effectively to change not only helps individuals cope with challenges but also positions organizations to capitalize on new opportunities and stay competitive in their industry.

Reader Action: Evaluate your organization's current level of resilience and adaptability through surveys or assessments, and identify areas for improvement.

Characteristics of Resilient Individuals

Resilient individuals possess certain characteristics that enable them to cope with challenges and adapt to change effectively. These traits include:

- **Optimism**: Resilient individuals maintain a positive outlook, even in the face of adversity. They believe in their ability to overcome challenges and view setbacks as opportunities for growth.
- **Emotional Regulation**: They can manage their emotions effectively, preventing negative feelings from overwhelming them. This allows them to stay focused and composed under pressure.
- **Self-efficacy**: Resilient people have confidence in their abilities and trust in their capacity to handle difficult situations. This self-belief drives them to take on challenges with determination.
- **Problem-solving Skills**: They are adept at identifying problems and finding solutions. Their critical thinking and creativity enable them to navigate obstacles efficiently.
- **Social Support**: Resilient individuals build strong networks of support. They seek help and advice from others, which helps them gain different perspectives and emotional support.

Example: Nelson Mandela is a prime example of resilience. Despite spending 27 years in prison, he emerged with a positive outlook and a commitment to reconciliation, ultimately leading South Africa to a peaceful transition from apartheid to democracy.

Insights: Resilience is not an inherent trait but a set of skills that can be developed and strengthened over time.

Reader Action: Reflect on your personal resilience traits and identify areas where you can improve. Consider setting specific goals to enhance these characteristics.

Techniques for Developing Resilience in the Workplace

Developing resilience in the workplace involves implementing various techniques and strategies. Here are some effective methods:

- **Mindfulness and Stress Management**: Encouraging mindfulness practices, such as meditation and deep breathing exercises, can help employees manage stress and stay focused. Research from Harvard Medical School shows that mindfulness can increase resilience by enhancing emotional regulation and reducing stress.
    - **Actionable Step**: Implement daily or weekly mindfulness sessions for employees, possibly led by trained professionals or through digital platforms like Headspace or Calm.
    - **Tip**: Create a quiet space in the office where employees can practice mindfulness or take a break from work pressures.
- **Cognitive Behavioral Techniques (CBT)**: CBT can help employees reframe negative thoughts and develop a more positive mindset. Training sessions on CBT techniques can be beneficial for fostering resilience.
    - **Actionable Step**: Offer workshops or online courses on CBT techniques. Partner with mental health professionals to provide these resources.
    - **Tip**: Encourage employees to keep a journal to track their thoughts and progress in adopting CBT techniques.
- **Goal Setting and Achievement**: Setting realistic and achievable goals helps employees build confidence and a sense of accomplishment. Regularly reviewing and celebrating progress can boost resilience.
    - **Actionable Step**: Implement a goal-setting framework like OKRs (Objectives and Key Results) to help employees set and achieve meaningful goals.
    - **Tip**: Celebrate both small and large achievements publicly to encourage a culture of recognition and accomplishment.
- **Building Strong Relationships**: Creating opportunities for team building and social interactions can strengthen support networks within the workplace. Activities such

as team-building exercises and social events can enhance camaraderie and resilience.

- **Actionable Step**: Organize regular team-building activities, both in-person and virtually, to foster stronger relationships among team members.
- **Tip**: Encourage cross-departmental projects and initiatives to build wider networks of support within the organization.

- **Leadership Support**: Leaders play a crucial role in fostering resilience. Providing consistent support, offering constructive feedback, and creating a positive work environment can significantly impact employees' resilience levels.
  - **Actionable Step**: Train leaders in emotional intelligence and resilience-building strategies. Provide them with the tools and resources to support their teams effectively.
  - **Tip**: Encourage leaders to lead by example by openly discussing their own resilience practices and challenges.

Example: At Airbnb, the company offers "Airbnb Resilience Training" for its employees. This program includes workshops on mindfulness, emotional intelligence, and stress management, helping employees build resilience and adaptability.

Insights: Regular training and development programs that focus on resilience can create a culture where employees feel supported and valued, which in turn can reduce turnover and increase engagement.

Reader Action: Implement regular resilience training programs and encourage participation across all levels of the organization.

Effective Programs, Practices, or Exercises

Several programs and practices have proven effective in developing resilience in the workplace:

- **The Penn Resilience Program**: Developed by the University of Pennsylvania, this program teaches resilience skills through cognitive-behavioral and social-emotional

learning techniques. It has been successfully implemented in various organizations
to improve employee well-being and performance.

- ○ **Actionable Step**: Partner with educational institutions like the University of
    Pennsylvania to bring resilience training programs to your organization.
- ○ **Tip**: Offer incentives for participation in these programs, such as professional
    development credits or bonuses.

- **Headspace for Work**: This program offers guided meditation and mindfulness
  sessions designed to reduce stress and build resilience. Companies like Google and
  LinkedIn have implemented Headspace for Work to support their employees' mental
  health.

  - ○ **Actionable Step**: Subscribe to Headspace for Work or similar platforms and
      provide employees with access to guided meditation sessions.
  - ○ **Tip**: Encourage employees to schedule regular mindfulness breaks into their
      workday.

- **The Resilience Institute**: This organization provides training programs that
  combine scientific research with practical tools to enhance resilience. Their
  programs focus on physical, emotional, and mental well-being, helping employees
  thrive in challenging environments.

  - ○ **Actionable Step**: Engage with The Resilience Institute to conduct workshops
      and training sessions tailored to your organization's needs.
  - ○ **Tip**: Follow up on these training sessions with regular refreshers and updates
      to keep resilience practices top of mind.

Example: At SAP, the "SAP Global Mindfulness Practice" program has been instrumental in
fostering resilience among employees. The program includes mindfulness training, stress
management workshops, and resilience-building exercises, leading to improved employee
well-being and productivity.

Insights: Programs that offer a holistic approach to resilience—addressing physical,
emotional, and mental aspects—are often the most effective.

Reader Action: Evaluate existing employee development programs and integrate comprehensive resilience training that includes elements of mindfulness, emotional intelligence, and physical well-being.

Case Studies and Examples

Microsoft: During the COVID-19 pandemic, Microsoft implemented a comprehensive resilience strategy that included regular virtual check-ins, access to mental health resources, and flexibility in work arrangements. This approach helped employees adapt to remote work and maintain productivity.

- **Actionable Step**: Implement regular virtual check-ins to maintain a connection with remote employees and provide ongoing support.
- **Tip**: Use video conferencing tools like Microsoft Teams or Zoom to facilitate these check-ins.

Unilever: Unilever's "Lamplighter" program focuses on enhancing employees' resilience through physical, emotional, and mental well-being initiatives. The program includes workshops on stress management, mindfulness training, and resilience-building activities. As a result, Unilever has seen a significant improvement in employee engagement and well-being.

- **Actionable Step**: Develop a similar comprehensive well-being program that addresses multiple aspects of employee health.
- **Tip**: Gather employee feedback to tailor the program to their specific needs and preferences.

Johnson & Johnson: The company's "Energy for Performance" program is designed to build resilience by focusing on physical, emotional, mental, and spiritual well-being. Employees participate in workshops that teach them how to manage their energy levels, improve focus, and enhance overall resilience. The program has been linked to increased productivity and reduced burnout rates.

- **Actionable Step**: Create workshops that teach employees how to manage their energy and prioritize well-being.
- **Tip**: Encourage employees to take regular breaks and engage in activities that recharge them, both physically and mentally.

Insights: Successful resilience programs often integrate multiple elements, including mental health support, physical wellness initiatives, and ongoing training.

Reader Action: Consider implementing a multi-faceted resilience program in your organization that addresses various aspects of employee well-being.

Action Points for Readers

To build resilience and adaptability in the workplace, consider the following action points:

- **Immediate Actions**:
  - **Encourage mindfulness practices among employees**: Provide resources and spaces for employees to practice mindfulness and stress management techniques.
  - **Implement regular check-ins to provide support and feedback**: Schedule regular one-on-one meetings to discuss challenges, provide feedback, and offer support.
  - **Offer access to mental health resources and counseling services**: Ensure employees have access to mental health professionals and support services.
- **Long-Term Strategies**:
  - **Develop and implement resilience training programs**: Partner with experts to create comprehensive resilience training that includes various techniques such as CBT, mindfulness, and emotional intelligence.
  - **Foster a supportive work environment with strong leadership**: Train leaders to recognize and support resilience-building efforts and to create a positive, inclusive work culture.

- ○ **Promote a culture of continuous learning and adaptability**: Encourage ongoing education and training to help employees adapt to new challenges and changes.

Considerations:

- **Inclusivity and Accessibility**: Ensure that resilience programs are inclusive and accessible to all employees, considering different needs and preferences.
- **Regular Evaluation**: Regularly evaluate the effectiveness of resilience initiatives and make necessary adjustments based on feedback and outcomes.
- **Employee Ownership**: Encourage employees to take ownership of their resilience and well-being by providing tools and resources for self-improvement.

Tips:

- **Lead by Example**: Demonstrate resilience and adaptability in your own behavior to inspire your team.
- **Celebrate Small Wins**: Recognize and reward employees' efforts to build resilience, no matter how small the achievements may seem.
- **Create a Safe Space**: Foster an environment where employees feel comfortable discussing their challenges and stressors without fear of judgment.

Notes:

- **Continuous Journey**: Resilience is a continuous journey, not a one-time achievement. Regular reinforcement and practice are necessary to maintain and enhance resilience.
- **Tailored Programs**: Tailor resilience programs to fit the specific needs and culture of your organization, ensuring they are relevant and effective.

Example Action Plan:

Month 1:

- **Introduce Mindfulness Sessions**: Promote them through internal communications and create a quiet space in the office for practice.
- **Conduct a Resilience Survey**: Assess current levels of resilience and identify areas for improvement.

Month 2-3:

- **Launch CBT Workshops**: Offer workshops or online courses on CBT techniques.
- **Implement Regular Check-ins**: Schedule one-on-one meetings and virtual support groups for remote employees.

Month 4-6:

- **Evaluate Program Impact**: Gather feedback and adjust programs based on employee responses.
- **Introduce Additional Resources**: Provide ongoing support and new resilience-building activities as needed.

Ongoing:

- **Celebrate Achievements**: Publicly recognize and reward employees' efforts.
- **Update Training Programs**: Regularly refresh training to keep resilience practices relevant and top of mind.

Conclusion

Building resilience and adaptability in the workplace is essential for navigating the complexities of today's work environment. By understanding the importance of resilience, recognizing its key characteristics, and implementing effective techniques and programs, organizations can enhance their employees' well-being and productivity. This section aims to provide a comprehensive guide for leaders and employees to foster resilience, offering insights, actionable strategies, and real-life examples to inspire and guide them on their journey.

Section 11

Technology and Stress: Finding Balance

Impact of Technology on Workplace Stress Levels

The use of technology in the workplace has become ubiquitous, bringing both benefits and challenges. While technology can enhance productivity and streamline operations, it can also contribute significantly to workplace stress. Here are some advanced statistics and data points that highlight the impact of technology on workplace stress levels:

- **Digital Overload**: A study by the American Psychological Association (APA) found that nearly 50% of workers feel overwhelmed by the constant stream of digital communication. This digital overload can lead to increased stress and burnout.
- **After-Hours Work**: According to a survey by Deloitte, 70% of employees feel they are expected to be available outside of regular working hours due to technology. This blurring of boundaries between work and personal life can exacerbate stress levels.
- **Tech Anxiety**: Research by the Anxiety and Depression Association of America (ADAA) indicates that 30% of workers experience anxiety related to the use of new technology. The pressure to quickly adapt to new tools and platforms can be a significant source of stress.
- **Productivity Paradox**: A report by McKinsey & Company highlights that while technology can boost productivity, it can also create distractions. Employees spend up to 28% of their workweek managing emails and interruptions, which can lead to stress and decreased productivity.
- **Workplace Communication**: According to a study by RescueTime, the average worker spends about 3 hours per day on work-related communication. This constant connectivity can prevent employees from focusing on deep work and lead to increased stress.

- **Mental Health**: The World Health Organization (WHO) has found that excessive use of digital devices can lead to "technostress," a modern disease of adaptation caused by an inability to cope with new technologies in a healthy manner. This can result in symptoms such as anxiety, mental fatigue, and depression.

Insights: Recognizing the dual nature of technology's impact is crucial. While it offers numerous advantages, it's essential to manage its use to prevent stress and burnout.

Guidance for Organizations:

- **Regular Surveys**: Conduct regular surveys to assess employees' feelings about technology use. This can help identify specific stressors and areas for improvement.
- **After-Hours Policies**: Implement policies to limit after-hours work communications to help employees maintain a clear boundary between work and personal life.
- **Training Programs**: Provide training to help employees adapt to new technologies without anxiety. This can include workshops, online courses, and one-on-one support.

Guidance for Individuals:

- **Mindful Tech Use**: Be mindful of your own tech use and take breaks to disconnect. Regularly stepping away from screens can help reduce stress.
- **Set Boundaries**: Establish personal boundaries for work-related communications outside of office hours. This can help prevent burnout and maintain work-life balance.
- **Seek Support**: If adapting to new technologies causes anxiety, seek training or support. Utilize available resources such as workshops or ask for help from colleagues.

Action Points:

1. Conduct regular surveys to assess employees' feelings about technology use.
2. Implement policies to limit after-hours work communications.
3. Provide training to help employees adapt to new technologies without anxiety.

4. Encourage employees to set personal boundaries and take regular breaks from technology.

Strategies for Managing Digital Overload

Managing digital overload involves adopting strategies that help employees navigate the digital landscape without feeling overwhelmed. Here are some effective strategies:

- **Digital Detox**: Encouraging periodic digital detoxes can help employees disconnect from their devices and recharge. This could involve setting aside specific times or days where digital communication is minimized.
  - **Example**: Volkswagen has implemented policies to limit email access after work hours, helping employees maintain a healthier work-life balance.
- **Prioritization Tools**: Using prioritization tools and techniques can help manage the influx of digital communication. Tools like Trello, Asana, and Microsoft Teams can help organize tasks and reduce the feeling of being overwhelmed.
  - **Example**: At Google, employees use the "Inbox Zero" method to manage their emails, aiming to keep their inboxes empty or near empty.
- **Setting Boundaries**: Establishing clear boundaries for digital communication can reduce stress. This includes defining specific times for checking emails and messages and creating "no-tech" zones or times.
  - **Example**: Intel has adopted "Quiet Time," a period during the day when employees are encouraged to work without interruptions from digital communications.
- **Mindfulness and Wellness Programs**: Incorporating mindfulness and wellness programs can help employees manage stress associated with digital overload. Techniques such as meditation and breathing exercises can be effective.
  - **Example**: Aetna offers mindfulness programs that have shown to reduce stress by 28% among participants.
- **Batch Processing**: Encourage employees to check emails and messages at designated times rather than continuously throughout the day to reduce distractions and increase productivity.

- ○ **Example**: Deloitte encourages employees to designate specific times to check and respond to emails, thereby minimizing interruptions.

Guidance for Organizations:

- **Encourage Digital Detox**: Encourage employees to adopt digital detox strategies and provide the necessary tools and resources to support their implementation.
- **Offer Training**: Offer training on prioritization tools and techniques to help employees manage their digital workload.
- **Set Clear Boundaries**: Establish and communicate clear boundaries for digital communication to reduce stress.

Guidance for Individuals:

- **Schedule Digital Detoxes**: Schedule regular digital detoxes and set specific times for checking emails to minimize stress.
- **Utilize Prioritization Tools**: Use prioritization tools like Trello or Asana to manage tasks effectively and reduce feeling overwhelmed.
- **Practice Mindfulness**: Practice mindfulness techniques such as meditation and deep breathing exercises to manage stress.

Action Points:

1. Implement digital detox policies and encourage regular breaks from technology.
2. Provide training on prioritization tools and techniques.
3. Establish and communicate clear boundaries for digital communication.
4. Promote batch processing to reduce constant distractions.

Using Technology as a Tool for Stress Reduction

While technology can be a source of stress, it can also be leveraged as a tool for stress reduction. Here are some advanced technologies and tools that can help reduce workplace stress:

- **Mindfulness Apps**: Apps like Headspace and Calm provide guided meditation and mindfulness exercises that can help employees manage stress and maintain mental well-being.
  - **Example**: LinkedIn offers its employees access to Headspace to help them manage stress and improve focus.
- **Health and Wellness Platforms**: Platforms like Virgin Pulse and Fitbit Wellness provide comprehensive health and wellness programs that encourage physical activity, healthy eating, and stress management.
  - **Example**: IBM uses Virgin Pulse to promote employee wellness, leading to improved health outcomes and reduced stress levels.
- **Virtual Reality (VR) for Relaxation**: VR technology can be used to create immersive relaxation experiences. Apps like TRIPP offer VR meditation and relaxation exercises that can help employees unwind.
  - **Example**: Accenture has implemented VR relaxation sessions to help employees manage stress and enhance well-being.
- **Telehealth Services**: Providing access to telehealth services can ensure that employees receive timely mental health support. Platforms like BetterHelp and Talkspace offer online therapy and counseling.
  - **Example**: Cisco offers its employees access to telehealth services, providing convenient mental health support.
- **Fitness Apps**: Apps like MyFitnessPal and Strava can help employees stay physically active, which is crucial for managing stress. These apps provide personalized fitness plans and track progress.
  - **Example**: Google encourages its employees to use fitness apps and provides incentives for achieving fitness goals.

Guidance for Organizations:

- **Promote Wellness Apps**: Encourage the use of mindfulness and fitness apps as part of a broader wellness strategy.

- **Implement Health Platforms**: Implement comprehensive health and wellness platforms to promote overall well-being.
- **Explore VR Technology**: Explore VR technology for relaxation and incorporate it into stress management programs.
- **Provide Telehealth Access**: Provide access to telehealth services for mental health support.

Guidance for Individuals:

- **Use Wellness Apps**: Explore and utilize wellness apps like Headspace and MyFitnessPal to manage stress and promote well-being.
- **Stay Active**: Incorporate fitness apps into daily routines to maintain physical health.
- **Seek Telehealth Services**: Utilize telehealth services for convenient access to mental health support.

Action Points:

1. Offer subscriptions to mindfulness apps and encourage their regular use.
2. Implement comprehensive health and wellness platforms to promote overall well-being.
3. Explore VR technology for relaxation and incorporate it into stress management programs.
4. Provide access to telehealth services for mental health support.
5. Promote the use of fitness apps to encourage physical activity.

Case Studies and Examples

Microsoft: During the COVID-19 pandemic, Microsoft implemented a comprehensive resilience strategy that included regular virtual check-ins, access to mental health resources, and flexibility in work arrangements. This approach helped employees adapt to remote work and maintain productivity.

- **Guidance for Organizations**: Implement regular virtual check-ins to maintain a connection with remote employees and provide ongoing support.

- **Guidance for Individuals**: Use video conferencing tools like Microsoft Teams or Zoom to stay connected with colleagues and seek support.

Unilever: Unilever's "Lamplighter" program focuses on enhancing employees' resilience through physical, emotional, and mental well-being initiatives. The program includes workshops on stress management, mindfulness training, and resilience-building activities. As a result, Unilever has seen a significant improvement in employee engagement and well-being.

- **Guidance for Organizations**: Develop a similar comprehensive well-being program that addresses multiple aspects of employee health.
- **Guidance for Individuals**: Participate actively in available wellness programs and provide feedback to improve them.

Johnson & Johnson: The company's "Energy for Performance" program is designed to build resilience by focusing on physical, emotional, mental, and spiritual well-being. Employees participate in workshops that teach them how to manage their energy levels, improve focus, and enhance overall resilience. The program has been linked to increased productivity and reduced burnout rates.

- **Guidance for Organizations**: Create workshops that teach employees how to manage their energy and prioritize well-being.
- **Guidance for Individuals**: Engage in workshops and apply learned techniques to daily routines.

Salesforce: Salesforce has implemented a "Wellness Reimbursement Program" that provides financial support for employees to pursue wellness activities such as gym memberships, fitness classes, and mindfulness programs. This initiative has helped reduce stress and improve overall employee well-being.

- **Guidance for Organizations**: Offer financial incentives or reimbursements for employees to participate in wellness activities.

- **Guidance for Individuals**: Take advantage of wellness reimbursement programs to engage in activities that promote health and reduce stress.

Insights: Successful resilience programs often integrate multiple elements, including mental health support, physical wellness initiatives, and ongoing training.

Reader Action: Consider implementing a multi-faceted resilience program in your organization that addresses various aspects of employee well-being.

Action Points for Readers

To build resilience and adaptability in the workplace, consider the following action points:

- **Immediate Actions**:
  - **Encourage mindfulness practices among employees**: Provide resources and spaces for employees to practice mindfulness and stress management techniques.
  - **Implement regular check-ins to provide support and feedback**: Schedule regular one-on-one meetings to discuss challenges, provide feedback, and offer support.
  - **Offer access to mental health resources and counseling services**: Ensure employees have access to mental health professionals and support services.
- **Long-Term Strategies**:
  - **Develop and implement resilience training programs**: Partner with experts to create comprehensive resilience training that includes various techniques such as CBT, mindfulness, and emotional intelligence.
  - **Foster a supportive work environment with strong leadership**: Train leaders to recognize and support resilience-building efforts and to create a positive, inclusive work culture.
  - **Promote a culture of continuous learning and adaptability**: Encourage ongoing education and training to help employees adapt to new challenges and changes.

Considerations:

- **Inclusivity and Accessibility**: Ensure that resilience programs are inclusive and accessible to all employees, considering different needs and preferences.
- **Regular Evaluation**: Regularly evaluate the effectiveness of resilience initiatives and make necessary adjustments based on feedback and outcomes.
- **Employee Ownership**: Encourage employees to take ownership of their resilience and well-being by providing tools and resources for self-improvement.

Tips:

- **Lead by Example**: Demonstrate resilience and adaptability in your own behavior to inspire your team.
- **Celebrate Small Wins**: Recognize and reward employees' efforts to build resilience, no matter how small the achievements may seem.
- **Create a Safe Space**: Foster an environment where employees feel comfortable discussing their challenges and stressors without fear of judgment.

Notes:

- **Continuous Journey**: Resilience is a continuous journey, not a one-time achievement. Regular reinforcement and practice are necessary to maintain and enhance resilience.
- **Tailored Programs**: Tailor resilience programs to fit the specific needs and culture of your organization, ensuring they are relevant and effective.

Example Action Plan:

Month 1:

- **Introduce Mindfulness Sessions**: Promote them through internal communications and create a quiet space in the office for practice.
- **Conduct a Resilience Survey**: Assess current levels of resilience and identify areas for improvement.

Month 2-3:

- **Launch CBT Workshops**: Offer workshops or online courses on CBT techniques.
- **Implement Regular Check-ins**: Schedule one-on-one meetings and virtual support groups for remote employees.

Month 4-6:

- **Evaluate Program Impact**: Gather feedback and adjust programs based on employee responses.
- **Introduce Additional Resources**: Provide ongoing support and new resilience-building activities as needed.

Ongoing:

- **Celebrate Achievements**: Publicly recognize and reward employees' efforts.
- **Update Training Programs**: Regularly refresh training to keep resilience practices relevant and top of mind.

Conclusion

Finding the right balance with technology in the workplace is essential for maintaining employee well-being and productivity. By understanding the impact of technology on stress, implementing strategies to manage digital overload, and using technology as a tool for stress reduction, organizations can create a healthier work environment. This section aims to provide a comprehensive guide for leaders and employees to navigate the digital landscape effectively, offering insights, actionable strategies, and real-life examples to inspire and guide them on their journey.

Section 12

Cultural and Organizational Influences on Stress

How Organizational Culture Affects Stress Levels

Organizational culture significantly influences employee stress levels. A positive, supportive culture can significantly reduce stress, while a negative, high-pressure environment can exacerbate it. Here are some advanced statistics and data points that demonstrate how organizational culture affects stress levels:

- **Employee Well-being and Productivity**: According to a study by Gallup, employees who work in positive work cultures are 59% less likely to experience burnout. This not only boosts their well-being but also enhances productivity by 41%.

- **Impact of Leadership**: Research by the American Psychological Association (APA) found that 75% of employees believe that their immediate supervisor is the most stressful part of their job. Effective leadership can thus play a pivotal role in reducing workplace stress.

- **Communication and Transparency**: A survey by Deloitte revealed that 62% of employees who feel their organization has transparent communication are less likely to be stressed. Open communication channels can mitigate misunderstandings and anxiety.

- **Work-Life Balance**: The World Health Organization (WHO) reports that workplaces with policies supporting work-life balance see a 23% reduction in stress-related health issues among employees.

- **Organizational Support**: The Society for Human Resource Management (SHRM) found that organizations with supportive cultures see a 67% reduction in employee turnover, indicating lower stress and higher job satisfaction.

Insights: Recognizing the dual nature of technology's impact is crucial. While it offers numerous advantages, it's essential to manage its use to prevent stress and burnout.

Guidance for Organizations:

- **Promote Transparency**: Foster a culture of open communication where employees feel heard and valued.
- **Supportive Leadership**: Train leaders to be empathetic and supportive, helping to create a positive work environment.
- **Encourage Work-Life Balance**: Implement policies that support flexible working hours and remote work options.

Guidance for Individuals:

- **Seek Clarity**: Engage in open communication with supervisors and peers to ensure clear understanding and expectations.
- **Set Boundaries**: Manage work-life balance by setting personal boundaries and utilizing available policies.
- **Communicate Needs**: Speak up about stressors and seek support from HR or leadership if necessary.

Action Points:

1. Conduct regular employee surveys to gauge stress levels and identify cultural stressors.
2. Implement leadership training programs focused on empathy and support.
3. Promote policies that encourage work-life balance and flexibility.
4. Encourage employees to communicate their needs and set personal boundaries.

Strategies for Promoting a Positive Work Culture

Creating a positive work culture requires deliberate strategies that promote employee well-being and satisfaction. Here are some effective strategies:

- **Recognition and Appreciation**: Recognizing and appreciating employees' efforts can boost morale and reduce stress. Regularly acknowledging accomplishments, both big and small, fosters a sense of value and belonging.

- - **Example**: Salesforce has a robust recognition program where employees can give and receive "thank you" badges, fostering a culture of appreciation.
- **Professional Development**: Offering opportunities for growth and development can increase job satisfaction and reduce stress. Employees who feel their skills are being enhanced are more likely to stay engaged and less likely to feel stressed.
  - **Example**: Google provides its employees with extensive professional development programs, including access to courses, workshops, and mentorship opportunities.
- **Health and Wellness Programs**: Implementing comprehensive wellness programs that address physical, mental, and emotional health can significantly reduce stress levels. These programs can include fitness activities, mental health support, and stress management workshops.
  - **Example**: Johnson & Johnson's "Energy for Performance" program focuses on holistic health, including physical, emotional, and mental well-being, leading to reduced stress and improved productivity.
- **Inclusive Policies**: Ensuring that workplace policies are inclusive and equitable helps in creating a supportive environment for all employees. This can involve promoting diversity, equity, and inclusion (DEI) initiatives.
  - **Example**: Microsoft has implemented various DEI initiatives, such as unconscious bias training and employee resource groups, to create a more inclusive and supportive work environment.

Guidance for Organizations:

- **Implement Recognition Programs**: Develop programs to regularly acknowledge and appreciate employee contributions.
- **Offer Development Opportunities**: Provide access to professional development and training programs.
- **Promote Health and Wellness**: Invest in comprehensive health and wellness programs that address various aspects of well-being.

- **Foster Inclusion**: Develop and implement DEI initiatives to ensure a supportive and inclusive work environment.

Guidance for Individuals:

- **Engage in Professional Development**: Take advantage of available training and development opportunities to enhance skills and reduce job-related stress.
- **Participate in Wellness Programs**: Actively engage in health and wellness programs offered by the organization.
- **Support Inclusivity**: Participate in and support DEI initiatives to contribute to a positive and inclusive work culture.

Action Points:

1. Develop and implement recognition and appreciation programs.
2. Offer a variety of professional development opportunities.
3. Invest in comprehensive health and wellness programs.
4. Implement and promote DEI initiatives.
5. Encourage employees to engage in professional development and wellness programs.

Diversity and Inclusion Initiatives in Stress Management

Diversity and inclusion (D&I) initiatives are crucial in creating a supportive work environment that reduces stress and fosters a sense of belonging. Effective D&I initiatives can address various stressors related to discrimination, bias, and lack of representation.

- **Inclusive Leadership**: Training leaders to understand and value diversity can create a more inclusive environment, reducing stress among underrepresented groups.
  - **Example**: Intel's Inclusive Leaders program trains leaders to recognize and mitigate biases, fostering a more inclusive and less stressful environment.
- **Employee Resource Groups (ERGs)**: ERGs provide support networks for employees from similar backgrounds or with shared interests, helping them navigate workplace challenges and reduce stress.

- ○ **Example**: Facebook has various ERGs, such as Women@, Black@, and Pride@, which offer support and resources to their members, contributing to a more inclusive culture.
- **Bias Training**: Conducting unconscious bias training can help employees recognize and address their biases, leading to a more inclusive and less stressful work environment.
  - ○ **Example**: Starbucks conducted nationwide unconscious bias training for all its employees to promote inclusivity and reduce workplace stress related to discrimination.
- **Mentorship Programs**: Establishing mentorship programs can provide guidance and support, helping employees from diverse backgrounds navigate their career paths and reduce stress.
  - ○ **Example**: PwC's mentorship program pairs junior employees with senior leaders to provide career guidance and support, fostering an inclusive environment.

Guidance for Organizations:

- **Train Leaders**: Implement inclusive leadership training programs to foster a supportive and inclusive culture.
- **Support ERGs**: Encourage the formation and active participation in ERGs to provide support and resources.
- **Conduct Bias Training**: Regularly conduct unconscious bias training to promote awareness and inclusivity.
- **Establish Mentorship Programs**: Create mentorship programs to provide guidance and support for employees from diverse backgrounds.

Guidance for Individuals:

- **Join ERGs**: Participate in or help establish ERGs that provide support and resources.
- **Engage in Training**: Actively participate in bias training and apply learnings to daily interactions.

- **Seek Mentorship**: Take advantage of mentorship programs to gain guidance and support.

Action Points:

1. Implement inclusive leadership training programs.
2. Encourage the formation and participation in ERGs.
3. Conduct regular unconscious bias training sessions.
4. Establish and promote mentorship programs.

Case Studies and Examples

Microsoft: Microsoft's comprehensive DEI initiatives have created a supportive environment that reduces stress and promotes well-being. Programs like unconscious bias training and employee resource groups have been instrumental in fostering an inclusive culture.

- **Guidance for Organizations**: Develop comprehensive DEI initiatives to create a supportive and inclusive work environment.
- **Guidance for Individuals**: Participate in DEI initiatives and support efforts to create an inclusive culture.

Unilever: Unilever's "Lamplighter" program focuses on enhancing employees' resilience through physical, emotional, and mental well-being initiatives. The program includes workshops on stress management, mindfulness training, and resilience-building activities, leading to improved employee engagement and well-being.

- **Guidance for Organizations**: Develop well-being programs that address various aspects of employee health.
- **Guidance for Individuals**: Engage actively in wellness programs and provide feedback for improvement.

Johnson & Johnson: The company's "Energy for Performance" program teaches employees how to manage their energy levels, improve focus, and enhance overall resilience. This holistic approach to employee well-being has been linked to increased productivity and reduced burnout rates.

- **Guidance for Organizations**: Create programs that address physical, emotional, and mental well-being.
- **Guidance for Individuals**: Apply the techniques learned in well-being programs to daily routines.

Starbucks: Starbucks' nationwide unconscious bias training aimed to promote inclusivity and reduce stress related to discrimination. This initiative helped create a more supportive environment for all employees.

- **Guidance for Organizations**: Conduct regular unconscious bias training to promote inclusivity.
- **Guidance for Individuals**: Participate in training sessions and advocate for inclusive practices.

Intel: Intel's Inclusive Leaders program trains leaders to recognize and mitigate biases, fostering a more inclusive and less stressful environment. This initiative has contributed to a more supportive culture and reduced stress among employees.

- **Guidance for Organizations**: Implement leadership training programs that focus on inclusivity and support.
- **Guidance for Individuals**: Engage in leadership training and support inclusivity efforts.

Facebook: Facebook's various ERGs, such as Women@, Black@, and Pride@, offer support and resources to their members, contributing to a more inclusive culture and reducing stress related to discrimination and bias.

- **Guidance for Organizations**: Support and promote the formation of ERGs.
- **Guidance for Individuals**: Participate in or help establish ERGs to create a supportive network.

Insights: Successful D&I initiatives and well-being programs often integrate multiple elements, including leadership training, support networks, and comprehensive health programs.

Reader Action: Consider implementing multi-faceted D&I initiatives and well-being programs that address various aspects of employee health and inclusivity.

Action Points for Readers

To build resilience and adaptability in the workplace, consider the following action points:

- **Immediate Actions**:
  - **Encourage mindfulness practices among employees**: Provide resources and spaces for employees to practice mindfulness and stress management techniques.
  - **Implement regular check-ins to provide support and feedback**: Schedule regular one-on-one meetings to discuss challenges, provide feedback, and offer support.
  - **Offer access to mental health resources and counseling services**: Ensure employees have access to mental health professionals and support services.
- **Long-Term Strategies**:
  - **Develop and implement resilience training programs**: Partner with experts to create comprehensive resilience training that includes various techniques such as CBT, mindfulness, and emotional intelligence.
  - **Foster a supportive work environment with strong leadership**: Train leaders to recognize and support resilience-building efforts and to create a positive, inclusive work culture.
  - **Promote a culture of continuous learning and adaptability**: Encourage ongoing education and training to help employees adapt to new challenges and changes.

Considerations:

- **Inclusivity and Accessibility**: Ensure that resilience programs are inclusive and accessible to all employees, considering different needs and preferences.
- **Regular Evaluation**: Regularly evaluate the effectiveness of resilience initiatives and make necessary adjustments based on feedback and outcomes.
- **Employee Ownership**: Encourage employees to take ownership of their resilience and well-being by providing tools and resources for self-improvement.

Tips:

- **Lead by Example**: Demonstrate resilience and adaptability in your own behavior to inspire your team.
- **Celebrate Small Wins**: Recognize and reward employees' efforts to build resilience, no matter how small the achievements may seem.
- **Create a Safe Space**: Foster an environment where employees feel comfortable discussing their challenges and stressors without fear of judgment.

Notes:

- **Continuous Journey**: Resilience is a continuous journey, not a one-time achievement. Regular reinforcement and practice are necessary to maintain and enhance resilience.
- **Tailored Programs**: Tailor resilience programs to fit the specific needs and culture of your organization, ensuring they are relevant and effective.

Example Action Plan:

Month 1:

- **Introduce Mindfulness Sessions**: Promote them through internal communications and create a quiet space in the office for practice.
- **Conduct a Resilience Survey**: Assess current levels of resilience and identify areas for improvement.

Month 2-3:

- **Launch CBT Workshops**: Offer workshops or online courses on CBT techniques.
- **Implement Regular Check-ins**: Schedule one-on-one meetings and virtual support groups for remote employees.

Month 4-6:

- **Evaluate Program Impact**: Gather feedback and adjust programs based on employee responses.
- **Introduce Additional Resources**: Provide ongoing support and new resilience-building activities as needed.

Ongoing:

- **Celebrate Achievements**: Publicly recognize and reward employees' efforts.
- **Update Training Programs**: Regularly refresh training to keep resilience practices relevant and top of mind.

Conclusion

Creating a positive organizational culture and implementing effective D&I initiatives are essential for maintaining employee well-being and productivity. By understanding the impact of organizational culture on stress, promoting strategies for a positive work culture, and leveraging D&I initiatives, organizations can foster a healthier and more inclusive work environment. This section aims to provide a comprehensive guide for leaders and employees to navigate cultural and organizational influences effectively, offering insights, actionable strategies, and real-life examples to inspire and guide them on their journey.

Section 13

Self-Care and Personal Well-being

Importance of Self-Care in Preventing Burnout

Self-care is essential for maintaining mental, emotional, and physical health, especially in high-stress environments. It helps prevent burnout, a state of chronic stress that leads to physical and emotional exhaustion. Here are some statistics and data points that demonstrate the importance of self-care in preventing burnout:

- **Burnout Prevalence**: According to a survey by Gallup, 76% of employees experience burnout on the job at least sometimes, with 28% feeling burned out "very often" or "always." Regular self-care practices can significantly reduce this prevalence.
- **Mental Health**: The American Psychological Association (APA) reports that 74% of adults have experienced stress levels so high that they felt overwhelmed or unable to cope. Self-care routines can mitigate these effects and improve mental health.
- **Productivity and Engagement**: Research by the World Health Organization (WHO) found that burnout can lead to a 50% reduction in productivity and a 37% increase in absenteeism. Implementing self-care strategies can enhance productivity and engagement.
- **Healthcare Costs**: The Global Wellness Institute estimates that workplace stress costs the U.S. economy more than $300 billion annually due to absenteeism, turnover, diminished productivity, and medical expenses. Effective self-care can reduce these costs by improving overall employee health.
- **Employee Retention**: According to a study by Kronos Incorporated, 95% of human resource leaders admit that employee burnout is sabotaging workforce retention, demonstrating the critical need for self-care practices to maintain a stable and healthy workforce.

Insights: Regular self-care is not just beneficial but essential for preventing burnout and maintaining overall well-being. Employers and employees alike should prioritize self-care to create a healthier, more productive work environment.

Guidance for Organizations:

- **Promote Work-Life Balance**: Encourage employees to take regular breaks, use their vacation time, and maintain a healthy work-life balance.
- **Provide Resources**: Offer access to self-care resources such as wellness programs, mental health services, and stress management workshops.
- **Encourage Flexibility**: Implement flexible working hours and remote work options to help employees manage their personal and professional lives more effectively.

Guidance for Individuals:

- **Prioritize Self-Care**: Make self-care a non-negotiable part of your routine, scheduling it as you would any other important activity.
- **Recognize Burnout Symptoms**: Be aware of the signs of burnout, such as chronic fatigue, irritability, and reduced performance, and take proactive steps to address them.
- **Utilize Available Resources**: Take advantage of wellness programs and mental health services offered by your employer.

Action Points:

1. Educate employees about the importance of self-care and how to integrate it into their daily routines.
2. Implement policies that support work-life balance and provide resources for self-care.
3. Encourage employees to recognize and address burnout symptoms early.

Practical Self-Care Strategies for Busy Professionals

For busy professionals, finding time for self-care can be challenging. However, integrating practical self-care strategies into daily routines can significantly improve well-being and prevent burnout. Here are some effective strategies:

- **Mindfulness and Meditation**: Practicing mindfulness and meditation can reduce stress and enhance focus. Apps like Headspace and Calm provide guided sessions that can be done in just a few minutes a day.
  - **Example**: At Google, employees are encouraged to participate in mindfulness programs, which have been shown to improve concentration and reduce stress.
- **Physical Activity**: Regular exercise is crucial for managing stress and improving overall health. Even short, daily workouts can make a significant difference.
  - **Example**: LinkedIn offers its employees access to on-site fitness centers and virtual workout sessions to promote physical well-being.
- **Healthy Eating**: Maintaining a balanced diet can help manage stress levels and boost energy. Busy professionals can benefit from planning meals and snacks in advance to ensure they make healthy choices.
  - **Example**: Salesforce provides healthy food options in its cafeterias and encourages employees to make nutritious choices.
- **Time Management**: Effective time management can reduce stress by helping professionals prioritize tasks and avoid feeling overwhelmed.
  - **Example**: Microsoft uses the "MyAnalytics" tool to help employees track their work habits and improve time management skills.
- **Social Connections**: Building and maintaining strong social connections can provide emotional support and reduce stress. Networking and engaging with colleagues can foster a supportive work environment.
  - **Example**: Slack encourages team-building activities and social events to strengthen employee connections.

Guidance for Organizations:

- **Encourage Mindfulness**: Promote mindfulness and meditation programs within the workplace.
- **Facilitate Physical Activity**: Provide access to fitness facilities and encourage regular physical activity.
- **Promote Healthy Eating**: Offer healthy food options and nutritional guidance.
- **Support Time Management**: Provide tools and training for effective time management.
- **Foster Social Connections**: Organize team-building activities and social events.

Guidance for Individuals:

- **Practice Mindfulness**: Integrate mindfulness practices into your daily routine to reduce stress.
- **Stay Active**: Incorporate physical activity into your schedule, even if it's just a short walk.
- **Eat Healthily**: Plan and prepare balanced meals and snacks.
- **Manage Time**: Prioritize tasks and use time management tools to stay organized.
- **Build Connections**: Engage with colleagues and build a support network.

Action Points:

1. Implement mindfulness and meditation programs in the workplace.
2. Provide access to fitness facilities and encourage regular exercise.
3. Offer healthy food options and nutritional guidance.
4. Provide time management tools and training.
5. Organize team-building activities and social events.

Creating a Personalized Self-Care Plan

A personalized self-care plan can help individuals manage stress and prevent burnout by addressing their unique needs and preferences. Here are the essential elements of creating a personalized self-care plan:

- **Self-Assessment**: Begin by assessing your current stress levels, lifestyle, and needs. Identify the areas of your life that need attention and improvement.
    - **Tool**: Use a self-care assessment tool or questionnaire to evaluate your well-being in different areas, such as physical health, emotional health, and social connections.
- **Set Goals**: Based on your self-assessment, set realistic and achievable self-care goals. These goals should be specific, measurable, and tailored to your needs.
    - **Example**: If you identify a need for better physical health, set a goal to exercise for 30 minutes, three times a week.
- **Develop a Plan**: Create a detailed plan outlining the specific actions you will take to achieve your self-care goals. Include a schedule and any resources you may need.
    - **Template**: Use a self-care plan template to organize your goals and actions. Include sections for physical, emotional, mental, and social self-care.
- **Implement and Monitor**: Put your self-care plan into action and regularly monitor your progress. Make adjustments as needed to ensure your plan remains effective and relevant.
    - **Tool**: Use a journal or digital app to track your progress and reflect on your self-care activities.
- **Seek Support**: Don't hesitate to seek support from friends, family, or professionals. They can provide encouragement and accountability as you work towards your self-care goals.
    - **Example**: Join a support group or find a self-care buddy to share your journey and stay motivated.

Guidance for Organizations:

- **Provide Resources**: Offer self-care assessment tools and templates to help employees create personalized self-care plans.
- **Support Implementation**: Encourage employees to develop and follow their self-care plans by providing time and resources.

Guidance for Individuals:

- **Conduct Self-Assessments**: Regularly assess your well-being and identify areas for improvement.
- **Set Realistic Goals**: Establish specific and achievable self-care goals.
- **Create a Detailed Plan**: Develop a comprehensive self-care plan with actionable steps.
- **Track Progress**: Monitor your progress and adjust your plan as needed.
- **Seek Support**: Reach out to others for support and accountability.

Action Points:

1. Provide self-care assessment tools and templates to employees.
2. Encourage employees to set realistic self-care goals and create detailed plans.
3. Support employees in implementing and monitoring their self-care plans.
4. Promote a culture of self-care and well-being in the workplace.

Case Studies and Examples

Google: Google's "gPause" mindfulness program encourages employees to practice mindfulness and meditation to reduce stress and improve focus. This initiative has helped many employees maintain their well-being and prevent burnout.

- **Guidance for Organizations**: Develop and promote mindfulness programs to support employee well-being.
- **Guidance for Individuals**: Participate in mindfulness programs and integrate practices into your daily routine.

LinkedIn: LinkedIn offers comprehensive wellness programs, including on-site fitness centers, virtual workout sessions, and mental health resources. These initiatives have significantly improved employee well-being and reduced stress.

- **Guidance for Organizations**: Provide access to wellness programs and facilities to support employee health.

- **Guidance for Individuals**: Engage in available wellness programs and prioritize physical activity.

Microsoft: Microsoft's "MyAnalytics" tool helps employees track their work habits and improve time management skills. By encouraging effective time management, Microsoft has helped employees reduce stress and enhance productivity.

- **Guidance for Organizations**: Implement tools and training to support effective time management.
- **Guidance for Individuals**: Use time management tools to prioritize tasks and stay organized.

Salesforce: Salesforce's "Healthy Food Initiative" provides healthy food options in its cafeterias and encourages employees to make nutritious choices. This initiative has promoted better eating habits and improved overall well-being.

- **Guidance for Organizations**: Offer healthy food options and nutritional guidance to employees.
- **Guidance for Individuals**: Make healthy eating a priority and plan nutritious meals and snacks.

PwC: PwC's mentorship program pairs junior employees with senior leaders to provide career guidance and support. This initiative has fostered a supportive work environment and reduced stress related to career development.

- **Guidance for Organizations**: Establish mentorship programs to provide guidance and support for employees.
- **Guidance for Individuals**: Seek mentorship opportunities to gain guidance and support in your career.

Facebook: Facebook encourages team-building activities and social events to strengthen employee connections. Their Employee Resource Groups (ERGs) offer support and resources to members, contributing to a more inclusive culture and reducing stress related to discrimination and bias.

- **Guidance for Organizations**: Support and promote the formation of ERGs and organize team-building activities.
- **Guidance for Individuals**: Participate in or help establish ERGs and engage in social events to build a support network.

Insights: Successful self-care initiatives often integrate multiple elements, including mindfulness, physical activity, healthy eating, time management, and social connections.

Reader Action: Consider implementing comprehensive self-care initiatives that address various aspects of employee well-being.

Action Points for Readers

To build resilience and adaptability in the workplace, consider the following action points:

- **Immediate Actions**:
    - **Encourage mindfulness practices among employees**: Provide resources and spaces for employees to practice mindfulness and stress management techniques.
    - **Implement regular check-ins to provide support and feedback**: Schedule regular one-on-one meetings to discuss challenges, provide feedback, and offer support.
    - **Offer access to mental health resources and counseling services**: Ensure employees have access to mental health professionals and support services.
- **Long-Term Strategies**:
    - **Develop and implement resilience training programs**: Partner with experts to create comprehensive resilience training that includes various techniques such as CBT, mindfulness, and emotional intelligence.
    - **Foster a supportive work environment with strong leadership**: Train leaders to recognize and support resilience-building efforts and to create a positive, inclusive work culture.

- **Promote a culture of continuous learning and adaptability**: Encourage ongoing education and training to help employees adapt to new challenges and changes.

Considerations:

- **Inclusivity and Accessibility**: Ensure that resilience programs are inclusive and accessible to all employees, considering different needs and preferences.
- **Regular Evaluation**: Regularly evaluate the effectiveness of resilience initiatives and make necessary adjustments based on feedback and outcomes.
- **Employee Ownership**: Encourage employees to take ownership of their resilience and well-being by providing tools and resources for self-improvement.

Tips:

- **Lead by Example**: Demonstrate resilience and adaptability in your own behavior to inspire your team.
- **Celebrate Small Wins**: Recognize and reward employees' efforts to build resilience, no matter how small the achievements may seem.
- **Create a Safe Space**: Foster an environment where employees feel comfortable discussing their challenges and stressors without fear of judgment.

Notes:

- **Continuous Journey**: Resilience is a continuous journey, not a one-time achievement. Regular reinforcement and practice are necessary to maintain and enhance resilience.
- **Tailored Programs**: Tailor resilience programs to fit the specific needs and culture of your organization, ensuring they are relevant and effective.

Example Action Plan:

Month 1:

- **Introduce Mindfulness Sessions**: Promote them through internal communications and create a quiet space in the office for practice.
- **Conduct a Resilience Survey**: Assess current levels of resilience and identify areas for improvement.

Month 2-3:

- **Launch CBT Workshops**: Offer workshops or online courses on CBT techniques.
- **Implement Regular Check-ins**: Schedule one-on-one meetings and virtual support groups for remote employees.

Month 4-6:

- **Evaluate Program Impact**: Gather feedback and adjust programs based on employee responses.
- **Introduce Additional Resources**: Provide ongoing support and new resilience-building activities as needed.

Ongoing:

- **Celebrate Achievements**: Publicly recognize and reward employees' efforts.
- **Update Training Programs**: Regularly refresh training to keep resilience practices relevant and top of mind.

Conclusion

Self-care is a critical component of maintaining personal well-being and preventing burnout. By understanding the importance of self-care, implementing practical strategies, and creating personalized self-care plans, individuals can enhance their resilience and overall health. Organizations play a vital role in supporting these efforts by providing resources and fostering a culture of well-being. This section aims to provide a comprehensive guide for leaders and individuals to prioritize self-care, offering insights, actionable strategies, and real-life examples to inspire and guide them on their journey.

Section 14

Legal and Ethical Considerations in Stress Management

Legal Rights and Protections Related to Workplace Stress

Legal rights and protections related to workplace stress are critical for ensuring that employees are treated fairly and have access to a safe working environment. Various laws and regulations address workplace stress and employee well-being. Here are some specific statistics and data points related to these legal rights and protections:

- **Occupational Safety and Health Administration (OSHA)**: According to OSHA, work-related stress is a significant factor in workplace accidents and injuries. Approximately 40% of workers report their job is very or extremely stressful.

- **Americans with Disabilities Act (ADA)**: The ADA provides protections for employees with mental health conditions, including stress and anxiety disorders. Under the ADA, employers must provide reasonable accommodations to employees with disabilities, which can include adjustments to work schedules or responsibilities to reduce stress.

- **Family and Medical Leave Act (FMLA)**: The FMLA entitles eligible employees to take up to 12 weeks of unpaid leave for serious health conditions, including mental health issues related to stress. This law helps protect employees' jobs while they address significant health concerns.

- **European Framework Agreement on Work-Related Stress**: This agreement recognizes that work-related stress can adversely affect health and safety and provides a framework for managing stress through risk assessment and preventive measures.

Studies and Surveys:

- A study published in the "Journal of Occupational Health Psychology" found that employees with access to stress management programs reported 24% lower stress levels and a 33% decrease in absenteeism.
- The International Labour Organization (ILO) highlights that workplace stress is linked to higher rates of cardiovascular disease, musculoskeletal disorders, and mental health issues, underscoring the need for legal protections and effective stress management strategies.

Guidance for Organizations:

- **Understand Legal Obligations**: Familiarize yourself with relevant laws and regulations, such as OSHA, ADA, and FMLA, to ensure compliance and protect employee rights.
- **Develop Stress Management Policies**: Create and implement policies that address workplace stress and promote employee well-being.
- **Train Managers**: Ensure that managers are trained to recognize signs of stress and understand the legal requirements for providing support and accommodations.

Guidance for Individuals:

- **Know Your Rights**: Understand your legal rights related to workplace stress and mental health conditions.
- **Seek Accommodations**: If needed, request reasonable accommodations from your employer to help manage stress and maintain your well-being.
- **Document Issues**: Keep records of any workplace stressors and your communications with management to support any potential legal claims.

Action Points:

1. Educate employees about their legal rights and protections related to workplace stress.
2. Develop and implement comprehensive stress management policies.

3. Ensure compliance with relevant laws and regulations to protect employee well-being.
4. Train managers to recognize and address workplace stress appropriately.

Ethical Responsibilities in Addressing Employee Well-Being

Employers have an ethical responsibility to ensure the well-being of their employees. This includes addressing workplace stress and creating a supportive environment. Here are some ethical principles and guidelines that emphasize the importance of addressing employee well-being:

- **Duty of Care**: Employers have a moral obligation to provide a safe and healthy work environment. This includes taking proactive steps to reduce workplace stress and support employees' mental health.
- **Fair Treatment**: Ethical treatment of employees involves recognizing the impact of stress on their well-being and ensuring they are treated with respect and fairness. This includes providing equal opportunities for all employees to access stress management resources and support.
- **Transparency and Communication**: Open and honest communication about workplace stress and well-being initiatives is essential. Employers should be transparent about the resources available to employees and encourage a culture of openness regarding mental health.
- **Employee Participation**: Involving employees in the development and implementation of stress management programs ensures that their needs and perspectives are considered. This participatory approach promotes a sense of ownership and engagement in well-being initiatives.

Ethical Frameworks and Standards:

- **The World Health Organization (WHO)**: The WHO's "Healthy Workplaces" framework emphasizes the importance of creating a supportive work environment that promotes physical and mental health.

- **The Global Reporting Initiative (GRI)**: GRI standards encourage organizations to report on their practices related to employee health and well-being, promoting transparency and accountability.

Guidance for Organizations:

- **Adopt Ethical Practices**: Implement ethical practices that prioritize employee well-being and address workplace stress.
- **Promote Transparency**: Communicate openly about stress management initiatives and resources available to employees.
- **Encourage Participation**: Involve employees in the development and implementation of stress management programs.
- **Provide Training**: Offer training programs that emphasize ethical considerations in managing workplace stress and promoting employee well-being.

Guidance for Individuals:

- **Engage in Well-Being Initiatives**: Actively participate in workplace well-being programs and provide feedback to help improve them.
- **Advocate for Fair Treatment**: Ensure you are being treated fairly and have access to the same well-being resources as your colleagues.
- **Communicate Openly**: Share your experiences and needs with your employer to help foster a culture of openness and support.

Action Points:

1. Adopt ethical practices that prioritize employee well-being.
2. Promote transparency and open communication about stress management initiatives.
3. Involve employees in the development and implementation of well-being programs.
4. Provide training on ethical considerations in stress management.

Compliance with Regulations and Policies

Compliance with regulations and policies related to workplace stress is essential for protecting employee well-being and avoiding legal liabilities. Here are some specific compliance requirements and policies that organizations should consider:

- **Occupational Safety and Health Administration (OSHA) Regulations**: Employers must comply with OSHA regulations that require a safe and healthy workplace. This includes addressing psychosocial hazards such as stress.
- **Americans with Disabilities Act (ADA) Compliance**: Ensure that reasonable accommodations are provided to employees with mental health conditions, including stress and anxiety disorders, as required by the ADA.
- **Family and Medical Leave Act (FMLA) Compliance**: Ensure that eligible employees can take leave for serious health conditions, including stress-related mental health issues, without fear of losing their jobs.
- **European Union (EU) Directives**: Organizations operating within the EU must comply with directives that address workplace stress, such as the European Framework Agreement on Work-Related Stress.

Examples of Successful Implementation:

- **SAP**: SAP has implemented comprehensive mental health programs that comply with legal requirements and promote employee well-being. Their initiatives include access to mental health resources, stress management workshops, and regular mental health assessments.
- **Deloitte**: Deloitte has established a well-being framework that includes compliance with relevant regulations and promotes a culture of well-being. Their programs offer support for mental health, flexible working arrangements, and wellness resources.

Guidance for Organizations:

- **Ensure Compliance**: Regularly review and update policies to ensure compliance with relevant regulations and laws.

- **Provide Training**: Offer training to managers and employees on legal rights, protections, and the importance of compliance.
- **Monitor and Evaluate**: Continuously monitor and evaluate stress management initiatives to ensure they meet legal and ethical standards.
- **Implement Reporting Mechanisms**: Establish clear procedures for employees to report stress-related issues and ensure that these reports are addressed promptly.

Guidance for Individuals:

- **Understand Policies**: Familiarize yourself with your organization's policies related to stress management and employee well-being.
- **Report Issues**: Report any non-compliance or concerns related to workplace stress to your HR department or relevant authority.
- **Seek Legal Advice**: If necessary, seek legal advice to understand your rights and protections under the law.

Action Points:

1. Regularly review and update stress management policies to ensure compliance with relevant regulations.
2. Provide training on legal rights and protections related to workplace stress.
3. Monitor and evaluate well-being initiatives to ensure they meet legal and ethical standards.
4. Implement reporting mechanisms for stress-related issues.

Case Studies and Examples

Google: Google's comprehensive well-being programs include compliance with legal requirements and a strong focus on employee mental health. Their initiatives, such as the Employee Assistance Program (EAP) and mental health resources, ensure employees have access to support and accommodations as needed.

- **Guidance for Organizations**: Develop and promote well-being programs that comply with legal requirements and provide comprehensive support for employee mental health.
- **Guidance for Individuals**: Utilize available well-being resources and support programs offered by your employer.

Unilever: Unilever's approach to managing workplace stress includes compliance with EU directives and ethical considerations. Their well-being programs focus on mental health support, flexible working arrangements, and regular well-being assessments.

- **Guidance for Organizations**: Implement well-being programs that comply with legal requirements and prioritize employee mental health.
- **Guidance for Individuals**: Engage in well-being programs and provide feedback to help improve them.

Johnson & Johnson: Johnson & Johnson's "Energy for Performance" program is designed to comply with legal requirements and promote employee well-being. The program includes stress management workshops, mental health resources, and support for work-life balance.

- **Guidance for Organizations**: Develop programs that comply with legal requirements and support employee well-being.
- **Guidance for Individuals**: Participate in stress management workshops and utilize available mental health resources.

PwC: PwC has implemented a well-being framework that includes compliance with relevant regulations and ethical practices. Their initiatives offer support for mental health, flexible working arrangements, and comprehensive wellness resources.

- **Guidance for Organizations**: Ensure compliance with legal requirements and promote ethical practices that prioritize employee well-being.
- **Guidance for Individuals**: Take advantage of flexible working arrangements and wellness resources offered by your employer.

Facebook: Facebook's Employee Resource Groups (ERGs) offer support and resources to members, contributing to a more inclusive culture and reducing stress related to discrimination and bias. Their comprehensive well-being programs also include compliance with legal requirements.

- **Guidance for Organizations**: Support and promote the formation of ERGs and ensure compliance with legal requirements.
- **Guidance for Individuals**: Participate in ERGs and engage in well-being programs to build a support network and reduce stress.

Insights: Successful stress management programs integrate legal compliance, ethical practices, and comprehensive support for employee well-being.

Reader Action: Consider implementing comprehensive stress management programs that address legal and ethical considerations and prioritize employee well-being.

Action Points for Readers

To effectively manage workplace stress, consider the following action points:

- **Immediate Actions**:
    - **Educate Employees on Legal Rights**: Provide training on legal rights and protections related to workplace stress.
    - **Implement Stress Management Policies**: Develop and implement policies that address workplace stress and promote employee well-being.
    - **Ensure Compliance with Regulations**: Regularly review and update policies to ensure compliance with relevant regulations.
- **Long-Term Strategies**:
    - **Develop Comprehensive Well-Being Programs**: Partner with experts to create well-being programs that include stress management, mental health support, and flexible working arrangements.

- ○ **Foster a Supportive Work Environment**: Train leaders to recognize and support stress management efforts and create a positive, inclusive work culture.
  - ○ **Promote Continuous Improvement**: Regularly evaluate well-being initiatives and make necessary adjustments based on feedback and outcomes.

Considerations:

- **Inclusivity and Accessibility**: Ensure that well-being programs are inclusive and accessible to all employees, considering different needs and preferences.
- **Regular Evaluation**: Regularly evaluate the effectiveness of stress management initiatives and make necessary adjustments based on feedback and outcomes.
- **Employee Ownership**: Encourage employees to take ownership of their well-being by providing tools and resources for self-improvement.

Tips:

- **Lead by Example**: Demonstrate commitment to well-being and stress management in your own behavior to inspire your team.
- **Celebrate Small Wins**: Recognize and reward employees' efforts to manage stress, no matter how small the achievements may seem.
- **Create a Safe Space**: Foster an environment where employees feel comfortable discussing their challenges and stressors without fear of judgment.

Notes:

- **Continuous Journey**: Stress management and well-being are continuous journeys, not one-time achievements. Regular reinforcement and practice are necessary to maintain and enhance well-being.
- **Tailored Programs**: Tailor stress management programs to fit the specific needs and culture of your organization, ensuring they are relevant and effective.

Example Action Plan:

Month 1:

- **Introduce Legal Rights Training**: Provide training on legal rights and protections related to workplace stress.
- **Conduct a Well-Being Survey**: Assess current levels of stress and well-being among employees and identify areas for improvement.

Month 2-3:

- **Launch Stress Management Workshops**: Offer workshops or online courses on stress management techniques.
- **Implement Regular Check-Ins**: Schedule one-on-one meetings and virtual support groups for remote employees.

Month 4-6:

- **Evaluate Program Impact**: Gather feedback and adjust programs based on employee responses.
- **Introduce Additional Resources**: Provide ongoing support and new well-being activities as needed.

Ongoing:

- **Celebrate Achievements**: Publicly recognize and reward employees' efforts.
- **Update Training Programs**: Regularly refresh training to keep well-being practices relevant and top of mind.

Conclusion

Legal and ethical considerations in stress management are critical for ensuring employee well-being and compliance with relevant regulations. By understanding legal rights and protections, implementing ethical practices, and complying with regulations, organizations can create a supportive work environment that reduces stress and promotes overall health.

This section aims to provide a comprehensive guide for leaders and employees to navigate legal and ethical considerations effectively, offering insights, actionable strategies, and real-life examples to inspire and guide them on their journey.

Section 15

Conclusion: Sustaining Well-being Beyond Work

Recap of Key Strategies for Mastering Stress at Work

As we conclude this comprehensive guide on managing workplace stress, it's essential to revisit the core strategies we've discussed. These strategies are designed to equip you with the tools and knowledge needed to thrive in both your professional and personal life.

1. **Understanding Workplace Stress:**
   - **Common Causes:** Workplace stress often stems from excessive workloads, tight deadlines, lack of support, and interpersonal conflicts. Recognizing these stressors is the first step in managing them effectively.
   - **Impacts:** Stress impacts productivity, mental health, and overall job satisfaction. By understanding its effects, you can better navigate and mitigate these challenges.

2. **The Science Behind Stress and Mental Health:**
   - **Psychological and Physiological Aspects**: Stress triggers a cascade of reactions in the body, affecting the brain, cardiovascular system, and immune function. Understanding these mechanisms helps in developing targeted stress management strategies.
   - **Neurological Effects:** Chronic stress can lead to structural and functional changes in the brain, impacting memory, decision-making, and emotional regulation.

3. **Effective Stress Management Techniques:**
   - **Immediate Relief:** Techniques such as deep breathing, progressive muscle relaxation, and short breaks can provide quick relief from acute stress.
   - **Long-term Approaches:** Incorporating regular physical activity, maintaining a balanced diet, and ensuring adequate sleep are vital for long-term stress management.

4. **Mindfulness and Meditation Practices:**
   - **Daily Routines:** Simple practices like mindful breathing, body scans, and mindful walking can be integrated into daily routines to reduce stress.
   - **Guided Meditations:** Using guided meditations can help focus the mind and foster a sense of calm and clarity.
5. **Effective Communication and Conflict Resolution:**
   - **Enhancing Communication Skills:** Clear and assertive communication helps in expressing needs and resolving misunderstandings, reducing stress from miscommunications.
   - **Constructive Conflict Resolution:** Techniques such as active listening, empathy, and finding common ground are essential for resolving conflicts and building supportive workplace relationships.
6. **Leadership's Role in Stress Management:**
   - **Creating Supportive Environments:** Leaders play a crucial role in fostering a supportive work environment by recognizing stressors and providing necessary resources.
   - **Training and Development:** Ongoing training for leaders on stress management and mental health awareness ensures they are equipped to support their teams effectively.
7. **Legal and Ethical Considerations in Stress Management:**
   - **Legal Protections:** Familiarity with laws such as OSHA, ADA, and FMLA is crucial for protecting employee rights and ensuring a safe workplace.
   - **Ethical Practices:** Implementing ethical practices that prioritize employee well-being fosters a positive and supportive work culture.

Encouragement for Continued Personal and Professional Growth

Sustaining well-being beyond work requires a commitment to continuous personal and professional growth. Here are some key principles to guide you on this journey:

1. **Lifelong Learning:**

- ○ **Opportunities for Growth:** Embrace opportunities for learning and development. Attend workshops, enroll in courses, and stay updated with industry trends to enhance your skills and knowledge.
  - ○ **Resilience and Adaptability:** Continuous learning helps you stay resilient and adaptable in a changing work environment, reducing stress and enhancing job satisfaction.

2. **Work-Life Balance:**
   - ○ **Setting Boundaries:** Establish clear boundaries between work and personal life. Avoid taking work home and set specific times for work-related tasks.
   - ○ **Prioritizing Self-Care:** Make self-care a priority by engaging in activities that rejuvenate you, such as hobbies, exercise, and spending time with loved ones.

3. **Personal Development Plans:**
   - ○ **Career and Well-being Objectives:** Create and follow a personal development plan that includes both career goals and personal well-being objectives. Regularly review and adjust your plan to stay aligned with your aspirations.

4. **Networking and Mentorship:**
   - ○ **Building Relationships:** Build a strong professional network to gain new perspectives, support, and opportunities for growth.
   - ○ **Seeking Mentorship:** Seek out mentors who can provide guidance, support, and advice on navigating your career and managing stress.

Final Thoughts on Achieving Balance and Success in the Workplace

Achieving balance and success in the workplace is an ongoing process that requires intentional effort and self-awareness. Here are some final thoughts to keep in mind:

1. **Self-Awareness and Reflection:**
   - ○ **Assessing Stress Levels:** Regularly assess your stress levels and identify triggers. Use tools such as stress diaries or apps to track your stress and its sources.

- Reflecting on Responses: Reflect on how you respond to stress and make necessary adjustments to your strategies. Practice self-compassion and avoid self-criticism.

2. **Resilience Building:**
   - **Developing Coping Mechanisms:** Cultivate resilience by developing healthy coping mechanisms such as problem-solving, positive thinking, and seeking social support.
   - **Maintaining a Positive Outlook:** Focus on maintaining a positive outlook and finding meaning in your work. Gratitude practices and positive affirmations can help shift your mindset.

3. **Support Systems:**
   - **Leveraging Support Networks:** Utilize your support networks, including family, friends, and professional colleagues. Don't hesitate to seek help when needed, whether it's through informal conversations or professional counseling.
   - **Creating a Supportive Environment:** Advocate for a supportive work environment where employees feel valued and heard. Encourage open communication and collaboration within teams.

4. **Mindfulness and Presence:**
   - **Practicing Mindfulness:** Practice mindfulness to stay present and focused. This helps you manage stress effectively and enhances your overall well-being.
   - **Mindful Activities:** Engage in mindful activities such as yoga, tai chi, or creative arts to promote relaxation and reduce stress.

Insights and Resources

Statistics and Data

- **Workplace Stress Impact:** According to the American Institute of Stress, 83% of US workers suffer from work-related stress, with 25% stating that their job is the number one stressor in their lives.

- **Cost of Stress:** The American Psychological Association estimates that workplace stress costs the US economy over $500 billion annually in lost productivity, healthcare costs, and absenteeism.

Case Studies and Examples

- **Google's Employee Well-being Programs:** Google offers extensive mental health resources, including the Employee Assistance Program (EAP) and mental health days, promoting a culture of well-being.
  - **Guidance for Organizations:** Develop and promote well-being programs that comply with legal requirements and provide comprehensive support for employee mental health.
  - **Guidance for Individuals:** Utilize available well-being resources and support programs offered by your employer.
- **Unilever's Mental Health Support:** Unilever's approach includes flexible working arrangements and regular well-being assessments, ensuring employees have access to necessary resources and support.
  - **Guidance for Organizations:** Implement well-being programs that comply with legal requirements and prioritize employee mental health.
  - **Guidance for Individuals:** Engage in well-being programs and provide feedback to help improve them.
- **Johnson & Johnson's "Energy for Performance" Program:** Designed to comply with legal requirements and promote employee well-being, this program includes stress management workshops, mental health resources, and support for work-life balance.
  - **Guidance for Organizations:** Develop programs that comply with legal requirements and support employee well-being.
  - **Guidance for Individuals:** Participate in stress management workshops and utilize available mental health resources.
- **PwC's Well-being Framework:** PwC has implemented a well-being framework that includes compliance with relevant regulations and ethical practices. Their initiatives

offer support for mental health, flexible working arrangements, and comprehensive wellness resources.

- o **Guidance for Organizations:** Ensure compliance with legal requirements and promote ethical practices that prioritize employee well-being.
- o **Guidance for Individuals:** Take advantage of flexible working arrangements and wellness resources offered by your employer.
- **Facebook's Employee Resource Groups (ERGs):** Facebook's ERGs offer support and resources to members, contributing to a more inclusive culture and reducing stress related to discrimination and bias. Their comprehensive well-being programs also include compliance with legal requirements.
  - o **Guidance for Organizations:** Support and promote the formation of ERGs and ensure compliance with legal requirements.
  - o **Guidance for Individuals:** Participate in ERGs and engage in well-being programs to build a support network and reduce stress.

Guidance for Sustaining Well-being Beyond Work

1. **Regular Self-Care Practices:**
   - o **Engage in Regular Physical Activity:** Regular exercise reduces stress, improves mood, and boosts overall health. Aim for at least 150 minutes of moderate aerobic activity or 75 minutes of vigorous activity each week.
   - o **Practice Mindfulness and Meditation:** Daily mindfulness practices enhance mental clarity and relaxation. Consider integrating activities like mindful breathing, body scans, and mindful walking into your routine.
   - o **Prioritize Adequate Sleep and Healthy Nutrition:** Ensure you get 7-9 hours of sleep per night and maintain a balanced diet rich in fruits, vegetables, and whole grains.

2. **Professional Development:**
   - o **Attend Workshops and Training Sessions:** Enhance your skills and knowledcdge by participating in relevant workshops and training sessions.

- ○ **Seek Opportunities for Career Advancement:** Actively look for opportunities to advance your career and take on new challenges.

3. **Work Environment Optimization:**
   - ○ **Advocate for a Healthy Work Environment:** Promote policies and practices that support a healthy work environment, such as flexible work arrangements and mental health resources.
   - ○ **Encourage Open Communication and Collaboration:** Foster a culture of open communication and teamwork within your organization.

Considerations for Organizations

1. **Inclusive Well-being Programs:** Develop programs that cater to the diverse needs of employees, ensuring accessibility and inclusivity.
2. **Regular Evaluation:** Continuously assess the effectiveness of well-being initiatives and make necessary adjustments.
3. **Employee Engagement:** Involve employees in the development and implementation of well-being programs to ensure they meet their needs and preferences.

Action Points for Readers

1. **Immediate Actions:**
   - ○ **Implement Stress Management Techniques:** Start using the stress management techniques discussed in this book.
   - ○ **Engage in Mindfulness Practices:** Incorporate mindfulness and meditation into your daily routine.
2. **Long-Term Strategies:**
   - ○ **Create a Personal Development Plan:** Outline your career goals and well-being objectives.
   - ○ **Foster a Supportive Network:** Build and maintain a strong professional and personal support network.

Example Action Plan

Month 1:

- **Self-Assessment:** Conduct a self-assessment to identify stressors and current coping mechanisms.
- **Set Goals:** Define clear personal and professional goals related to stress management and well-being.

Month 2-3:

- **Implement Strategies:** Begin practicing stress management techniques and mindfulness exercises.
- **Seek Support:** Join support groups or seek mentorship for additional guidance and motivation.

Month 4-6:

- **Evaluate Progress:** Assess the effectiveness of the implemented strategies and make necessary adjustments.
- **Expand Knowledge:** Attend workshops or training sessions to learn new stress management techniques.

Conclusion

Sustaining well-being beyond work is a continuous journey that involves commitment, self-awareness, and proactive effort. By applying the strategies and insights provided in this book, you can achieve balance and success in the workplace while nurturing your overall well-being. Remember, the key to mastering stress lies in understanding its causes, implementing effective management techniques, and fostering a supportive environment both at work and in your personal life. Keep striving for growth, balance, and well-being, and you will find success in all areas of your life.

Concluding Section

Final Thoughts and Call to Action

Final Thoughts and Call to Action

As we reach the end of this journey through the complexities and challenges of workplace stress, it's vital to reflect on the knowledge we've gained and how it can be applied to foster a healthier, more productive work environment. Stress is an inevitable part of professional life, but with the right tools and strategies, it can be managed effectively. This book has equipped you with a comprehensive understanding of stress, its impacts, and how to mitigate its effects to enhance both personal and professional well-being.

Call to Action: Your journey toward mastering stress doesn't end here. It's a continuous process of learning, adapting, and growing. Take the insights and strategies shared in this book and make a commitment to prioritize your mental health and well-being. Share these learnings with colleagues, advocate for supportive workplace practices, and be an active participant in creating a healthier work culture.

Summary of the Book's Key Insights and Takeaways

1. Understanding Workplace Stress:

- **Common Causes and Impacts:** Workplace stress stems from excessive workloads, tight deadlines, and interpersonal conflicts. It has far-reaching effects on productivity, mental health, and job satisfaction, often leading to burnout and high turnover rates.
- **Impact on Productivity:** Stress negatively impacts concentration, decision-making, and overall job performance. Chronic stress can lead to absenteeism and presenteeism, where employees are physically present but mentally disengaged.

2. The Science Behind Stress and Mental Health:

- **Psychological and Physiological Effects:** Stress affects the brain, cardiovascular system, and immune function. Chronic stress can lead to significant changes in brain structure and function, such as shrinking the prefrontal cortex and enlarging the amygdala, which increases anxiety and fear responses.
- **Neurological Impact:** Prolonged stress can cause neural connections in the brain to deteriorate, affecting memory and cognitive function. Understanding these effects underscores the importance of effective stress management.

3. Effective Stress Management Techniques:

- **Immediate and Long-term Approaches:** Techniques like deep breathing, progressive muscle relaxation, regular physical activity, and balanced nutrition are crucial for managing stress. Long-term approaches include setting realistic goals, time management, and seeking professional support when needed.
- **Proven Strategies:** Regular exercise, adequate sleep, and a healthy diet are foundational to stress management. Cognitive-behavioral strategies, such as reframing negative thoughts, can also be highly effective.

4. Mindfulness and Meditation Practices:

- **Daily Integration:** Incorporating mindfulness into daily routines through practices like mindful breathing, body scans, and guided meditations can significantly reduce stress levels. These practices enhance self-awareness and emotional regulation.
- **Benefits of Mindfulness:** Mindfulness practices improve focus, reduce emotional reactivity, and enhance overall well-being. Studies have shown that regular mindfulness practice can decrease symptoms of anxiety and depression.

5. Effective Communication and Conflict Resolution:

- **Enhancing Skills and Constructive Approaches:** Clear, assertive communication and constructive conflict resolution are essential for reducing workplace stress and building supportive relationships. Effective communication fosters a collaborative work environment.

- **Strategies for Conflict Resolution:** Active listening, empathy, and problem-solving techniques help address conflicts constructively. Creating a culture of open communication can prevent conflicts from escalating.

6. Leadership's Role in Stress Management:

- **Creating Supportive Environments:** Leaders play a critical role in fostering a supportive work environment and providing necessary resources for stress management. Leadership development programs can enhance leaders' ability to support their teams effectively.
- **Leadership Training:** Training programs for leaders on stress management, emotional intelligence, and supportive communication are crucial. Leaders should model healthy behaviors and encourage a culture of well-being.

7. Legal and Ethical Considerations:

- **Understanding Protections and Responsibilities:** Familiarity with laws such as OSHA, ADA, and FMLA is essential for protecting employee rights and ensuring a safe workplace. Ethical considerations involve creating a fair and supportive environment for all employees.
- **Compliance and Best Practices:** Organizations must ensure compliance with legal standards while promoting ethical practices. This includes providing reasonable accommodations and fostering an inclusive work environment.

8. Conclusion: Sustaining Well-being Beyond Work:

- **Commitment to Growth and Balance:** Continuous personal and professional development, establishing work-life boundaries, and leveraging support systems are key to long-term well-being. Sustaining well-being requires ongoing effort and adaptation.
- **Lifelong Learning:** Embrace opportunities for continuous learning and growth. Engage in activities that promote personal and professional development, and seek balance in all aspects of life.

Empowering Readers to Prioritize Their Mental Health and Well-being

Empowerment starts with recognizing that your mental health and well-being are paramount. Here are some empowering steps to take:

1. Self-Awareness and Reflection:

- Regularly assess your stress levels and triggers. Use tools like journals or stress assessment scales to track your stress and identify patterns.
- Reflect on your responses to stress and adjust your strategies as needed. Understand which techniques work best for you and make them a regular part of your routine.

2. Resilience and Adaptability:

- Develop healthy coping mechanisms and maintain a positive outlook. Practices such as gratitude journaling and positive affirmations can enhance resilience.
- Embrace opportunities for growth and stay adaptable to changes. Flexibility and openness to change are key components of resilience.

3. Building Support Networks:

- Utilize your support networks, including family, friends, and professional colleagues. Engage in regular social activities and seek support when needed.
- Advocate for and participate in workplace well-being programs. Encourage your organization to prioritize mental health initiatives and provide feedback to improve them.

4. Continuous Learning:

- Engage in lifelong learning to enhance your skills and knowledge. Pursue professional development opportunities and stay informed about the latest research on stress management.

- Seek mentorship and guidance to navigate your career and manage stress. Mentors can provide valuable insights and support in your professional journey.

Actionable Steps for Implementing Strategies Learned from the Book

Immediate Actions:

- **Practice Stress Management Techniques:** Start using techniques like deep breathing, progressive muscle relaxation, and mindfulness exercises. Incorporate these practices into your daily routine to build resilience.
- **Engage in Physical Activity:** Incorporate regular physical activity into your routine. Exercise is a powerful stress reducer and enhances overall well-being.

Long-term Strategies:

- **Create a Personal Development Plan:** Outline your career goals and well-being objectives. Set achievable milestones and regularly review your progress.
- **Foster a Supportive Network:** Build and maintain strong professional and personal support networks. Engage in regular networking and seek out supportive relationships.
- **Advocate for Healthy Work Environments:** Promote policies and practices that support mental health and well-being in your workplace. Encourage open communication and provide feedback to improve workplace practices.

Example Action Plan:

Month 1:

- **Self-Assessment:** Identify stressors and current coping mechanisms. Use tools like the Perceived Stress Scale (PSS) to gauge your stress levels.
- **Set Goals:** Define clear personal and professional goals related to stress management and well-being. Create a vision board or write down your goals to keep them in focus.

Month 2-3:

- **Implement Strategies:** Begin practicing stress management techniques and mindfulness exercises. Start small and gradually increase the frequency and duration of these practices.
- **Seek Support:** Join support groups or seek mentorship for additional guidance and motivation. Consider finding a stress management coach or therapist if needed.

Month 4-6:

- **Evaluate Progress:** Assess the effectiveness of the implemented strategies and make necessary adjustments. Use feedback from your journal or stress assessments to refine your approach.
- **Expand Knowledge:** Attend workshops or training sessions to learn new stress management techniques. Stay informed about the latest research and best practices in stress management.

Final Reflections

Mastering stress at work is a dynamic and ongoing journey. By understanding stress and implementing the strategies discussed in this book, you are well-equipped to navigate the challenges of the workplace while maintaining your mental health and well-being. Remember, the key to success lies in continuous learning, self-awareness, and a proactive approach to managing stress. Embrace this journey with confidence and commit to prioritizing your well-being every step of the way.

Final Thoughts and Call to Action

The journey doesn't end here. To truly master stress at work, continuous effort and commitment are required. Here are some final thoughts and actionable steps to help you maintain and enhance your well-being beyond the workplace:

Final Thoughts

1. Recap of Key Strategies for Mastering Stress at Work:

- Effective stress management techniques, mindfulness practices, and strong communication skills are essential tools.
- Leadership plays a crucial role in fostering a supportive environment and promoting well-being.
- Legal and ethical considerations ensure a fair and safe workplace, emphasizing the importance of compliance and ethical practices.

2. Encouragement for Continued Personal and Professional Growth:

- Lifelong learning and adaptability are key to personal and professional development. Embrace opportunities for growth and stay resilient in the face of challenges.
- Building and maintaining supportive relationships, both professionally and personally, is vital for long-term well-being.

3. Final Thoughts on Achieving Balance and Success in the Workplace:

- Achieving balance involves setting boundaries, prioritizing self-care, and leveraging support systems.
- Success in the workplace is not just about professional achievements but also about maintaining overall well-being and fostering a positive work environment.

Call to Action

1. Empowerment:

- Prioritize your mental health and well-being. Make a commitment to incorporate stress management practices into your daily routine.
- Advocate for supportive workplace practices and be an active participant in creating a healthier work culture.

2. Implementation:

- Start with immediate actions, such as practicing stress management techniques and engaging in regular physical activity.
- Develop a long-term personal development plan and continuously evaluate your progress.

3. Advocacy:

- Encourage your organization to prioritize mental health initiatives and provide feedback to improve them.
- Share your learnings and experiences with colleagues to promote a supportive and healthy work environment.

4. Continuous Learning:

- Stay informed about the latest research and best practices in stress management.
- Engage in professional development opportunities and seek mentorship for ongoing guidance and support.

Concluding Thoughts

Mastering stress at work is a continuous journey of learning, growth, and adaptation. By embracing the strategies and insights shared in this book, you are well-equipped to navigate the challenges of the workplace while maintaining your mental health and well-being. Remember, the key to success lies in continuous learning, self-awareness, and a proactive approach to managing stress. Embrace this journey with confidence and commit to prioritizing your well-being every step of the way. Your mental health and well-being are paramount, and by prioritizing them, you can achieve balance, success, and fulfillment in both your professional and personal life.

Final Empowerment

The power to master stress at work lies within you. Take the knowledge and tools from this book, apply them diligently, and watch as your work life transforms into a more balanced, fulfilling, and productive experience. Remember, the journey is ongoing, and every step you take towards managing stress is a step towards a healthier, happier, and more successful you.

Commit to this journey, advocate for yourself and others, and be the catalyst for positive change in your workplace. Your mental health and well-being are worth it, and with the right strategies, you can create a work environment that supports and nurtures both your professional ambitions and personal fulfillment.

www.ingramcontent.com/pod-product-compliance
Lightning Source LLC
Chambersburg PA
CBHW081213260726
48653CB00010BA/3631